Living Through the Korean War

Other Books in the Living Through the Cold War series:

Living Through the Korean War

Charles W. Carey Jr., Book Editor

GREENHAVEN PRESS
An imprint of Thomson Gale, a part of The Thomson Corporation

THOMSON
———✳———™
GALE

Detroit • New York • San Francisco • San Diego • New Haven, Conn.
Waterville, Maine • London • Munich

Bonnie Szumski, *Publisher*
Helen Cothran, *Managing Editor*
Scott Barbour, *Series Editor*

© 2006 Thomson Gale, a part of The Thomson Corporation.

For more information, contact:
Greenhaven Press
27500 Drake Rd.
Farmington Hills, MI 48331-3535
Or you can visit our Internet site at http://www.gale.com

LIBRARY OF CONGRESS CATALOGING-IN-PUBLICATION DATA

Living through the Korean War / Charles W. Carey Jr., book editor
p. cm. -- (Living through the Cold War)
   Includes bibliographical references and index. 0-7377-2911-2 (lib. : alk. paper)
  1. Korean War, 1950–1953--United States. 2. Korean War, 1950–1953. I. Carey, Charles W. II. Series.
  DS919.L57 2006
  951.904'2--dc22

                                                  2005055021

Contents

Foreword

At the midpoint of the Cold War, in early 1968, U.S. television viewers saw surprising reports from Vietnam, where American ground troops had been fighting since 1965. They learned that South Vietnamese Communist rebels, known as the Vietcong, had attacked unexpectedly throughout the country. At one point Vietcong insurgents engaged U.S. troops and officials in a firefight at the very center of U.S. power in Vietnam, the American embassy in South Vietnam's capital, Saigon. Meanwhile, thousands of soldiers and marines faced a concerted siege at Khe Sanh, an isolated base high in central Vietnam's mountains. Their adversary was not the Vietcong, but rather the regular North Vietnamese army.

Reporters and U.S. citizens quickly learned that these events constituted the Tet Offensive, a coordinated attack by Vietnamese Communists that occurred in late January, the period of Tet, Vietnam's new year. The American public was surprised by the Tet Offensive because they had been led to believe that the United States and its South Vietnamese allies were winning the war, that Vietcong forces were weak and dwindling, and that the massive buildup of American forces (there were some five hundred thousand U.S. troops in Vietnam by early 1968) ensured that the south would remain free of a Communist takeover. Since 1965, politicians, pundits, and generals had claimed that massive American intervention was justified and that the war was being won. On a publicity tour in November 1967 General William Westmoreland, the American commander in Vietnam, had assured officials and reporters that "the ranks of the Vietcong are thinning steadily" and that "we have reached a point where the end begins to come into view." President Lyndon B. Johnson's advisers, meanwhile, continually encouraged him to publicly emphasize "the light at the end of the tunnel."

Ordinary Americans had largely supported the troop buildup in Vietnam, believing the argument that the country was an important front in the Cold War, the global effort to stop the spread of communism that had begun in the late 1940s. Communist regimes already held power in nearby China, North Korea, and in northern Vietnam; it was deemed necessary to hold the line in the south not only to prevent communism from taking hold there but to prevent other nations from falling to communism throughout Asia. In 1965, polls showed that 80 percent of Americans believed that intervention in Vietnam was justified despite the fact that involvement in this fight would alter American life in numerous ways. For example, young men faced the possibility of being drafted and sent to fight—and possibly die—in a war thousands of miles away. As the war progressed, citizens watched more and more of their sons—both draftees and enlisted men—being returned to the United States in coffins (approximately fifty-eight thousand Americans died in Vietnam). Antiwar protests roiled college campuses and sometimes the streets of major cities. The material costs of the war threatened domestic political reforms and America's economic health, offering the continuing specter of rising taxes and shrinking services. Nevertheless, as long as the fight was succeeding, a majority of Americans could accept these risks and sacrifices.

Tet changed many minds, suggesting as it did that the war was not, in fact, going well. When CBS news anchor Walter Cronkite, who was known as "the most trusted man in America," suggested in his broadcast on the evening of February 27 that the Vietnam War might be unwinnable and could only end in a stalemate, many people wondered if he might be right and began to suspect that the positive reports from generals and politicians might have been misleading. It was a turning point in the battle for public opinion. Johnson reportedly said that Cronkite's expressions of doubt signaled the loss of mainstream America's support for the war. Indeed, after Tet more and more people joined Cronkite in wondering whether fighting this obscure enemy in an isolated country halfway around the world was worth the cost—whether it was a truly important front in the Cold War. They made their views known through demonstrations and opinion polls, and politicians were forced to respond. In a dramatic and unexpected turn of events, Johnson declined to run for reelection in 1968, stating that his involvement in the political campaign would detract from his efforts to negotiate a peace agreement with North Vietnam. His successor, Richard Nixon, won the election after promising to end the war.

The Tet Offensive and its consequences provide strong examples of how the Cold War touched the lives of ordinary Americans. Far from being an abstract geopolitical event, the Cold War, as Tet reveals, was an ever-present influence in the everyday life of the nation. Greenhaven Press's Living Through the Cold War series provides snapshots into the lives of ordinary people during the Cold War, as well as their reactions to its major events and developments. Each volume is organized around a particular event or distinct stage of the Cold War. Primary documents such as eyewitness accounts and speeches give firsthand insights into both ordinary peoples' experiences and leaders' decisions. Secondary sources provide factual information and place events within a larger global and historical context. Additional resources include a detailed introduction, a comprehensive chronology, and a thorough bibliography. Also included are an annotated table of contents and a detailed index to help the reader locate information quickly. With these features, the Living Through the Cold War series reveals the human dimension of the superpower rivalry that defined the globe during most of the latter half of the twentieth century.

Introduction

The United States and the Soviet Union were allies during World War II, but their wartime partnership barely outlasted that global conflict. No sooner did WWII hostilities end than the world's two superpowers became enemies in the forty-six-year struggle known as the Cold War. Their complex antagonism originated in deep ideological differences: The USSR was founded on communism, the United States (and other Western democracies) on capitalism, two opposing political and economic systems that experts on both sides argued could not peacefully coexist. The two superpowers struggled to extend their political and military influence over the rest of the world both to safeguard their respective ways of life and to win adherents to their respective systems, each believing its own would ultimately prevail. Every gain for one side was viewed as a loss for the other, so both superpowers essentially had interests to protect everywhere—and opportunities to advance everywhere—in the destabilization that characterized the immediate postwar world. No place represented these interests and opportunities better than Korea, the mountainous peninsula in East Asia where Cold War animosity erupted in armed conflict in 1950.

Korea Loses Its Independence

The immediate cause of the Korean War was Korean nationalism—the Korean people's desire to be independent and unified. Until the late nineteenth century the small country had managed to remain independent from its powerful neighbors, China and Japan. Then in 1894 Japanese troops forced the Korean government to recognize Japanese hegemony over Korea via the Treaty of Shimonoseki. Eleven years later the Treaty of Portsmouth, an international agreement that ended a war between Russia and Japan, made Korea a Japanese protectorate. The last vestiges of Korean independence were erased in 1910 when Japan annexed Korea, and for the next thirty-five years Korea was essentially a Japanese colony.

Koreans were ruthlessly oppressed by the Japanese, especially during the late 1930s and early 1940s, when Japan went to war first with China and then with the United States. Hundreds of thousands of Korean men were drafted into the Japanese armed forces or forced to serve as laborers in mines, factories, and military bases, and Koreans' hatred of the Japanese intensified when thousands of Korean women were forced into service as sex slaves for Japanese soldiers and sailors. A Korean provisional government in exile was established in China, and in 1942 a liberation army of Korean freedom fighters declared war on Japan and fought against the Japanese from bases in China and the Soviet Union.

Despite Koreans' suffering and their brutal experience during the war, Korean society was as homogeneous as it had ever been. Most Koreans were descended from the same ethnic stock and spoke the same language. Although there was little uniformity of religious belief, a majority of women were Buddhists while a majority of men were Confucians. As the prospect of throwing off their Japanese masters neared, however, Koreans were increasingly divided over what kind of economy to establish for themselves. A majority of the Korean freedom fighters, especially those from the north, favored socialism and strict state control, mostly through the influence of their Communist Soviet allies. Meanwhile, many members of the new government favored capitalism, through the influence of American forces fighting against the Japanese from bases in Southeast Asia. However, differences of opinion concerning economic systems were overshadowed by Koreans' single-minded desire to be unified and once again independent.

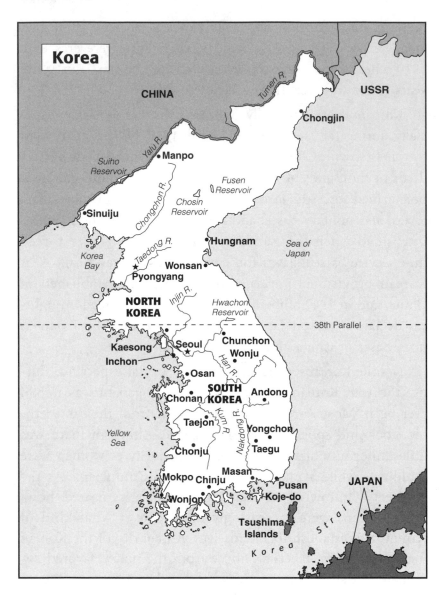

Korea Is Divided

But unity was not to be. With the defeat of Japan inevitable, three days after the Soviets officially entered the war against the Japanese on August 8, 1945, the United States issued General Order No. 1. This order was directed at Japanese troops in Korea who wished to surrender to the Allies; it instructed troops north of the 38th parallel, which divides the Korean peninsula roughly in half, to surrender to the Soviets, while troops south of the 38th parallel were to surrender to the Americans. Experts debate the real reason for this order. Some claim that it was intended simply to expedite the surrender of Japanese forces in Korea, while others argue that its purpose was to prevent the Soviets from taking over all of Korea before the Americans could reach the peninsula. In fact, U.S. troops did not enter Korea until September 1945, a month after Soviet troops arrived, giving weight to the latter interpretation. Whatever its underlying purpose, General Order No. 1 divided Koreans into two opposing camps, with disastrous results.

Both superpowers stationed troops in Korea for several years after the Japanese surrender. Soviet troops in the north supported the establishment of a pro-Soviet regime led by Kim Il Sung, who had served as a major in the Soviet army during World War II. Meanwhile, U.S. troops supported the temporary U.S. military administration and, after 1948, propped up a pro-American regime led by Syngman Rhee, former president of the Korean government in exile. In time, the two camps became known as the Democratic People's Republic of Korea (DPRK), or North Korea, and the Republic of Korea (ROK), or South Korea.

Koreans Seek Reunification

The unification movement was still alive, but by 1948 the issue of unification was entangled in the larger issues of the Cold War. Neither side was able or willing to compromise for fear of weakening its own position or giving political advantage to the other. The United Nations Temporary Commission on Korea stepped in and arranged for democratic elections to take place in Korea in 1948, but the result (the election of a national assembly loyal to Rhee) was accepted only in the south, the north having elected a pro-Communist assembly loyal to Kim a year earlier. Over the next year American troops were withdrawn from Korea despite Kim's ominous declaration in September 1948 that North Korea had jurisdiction over the entire country.

Kim's primary objective was not to spread global communism. Rather, it was to reunify Korea, North and South, under one government. Thus, when Kim began the Korean War on June 25, 1950, by ordering an estimated 135,000 troops of the North Korean People's Army (NKPA) to invade South Korea, he began a civil war. The United States, however, did not view the conflict in this way. President Harry S. Truman adamantly maintained that North Korea's invasion of South Korea was another attempt by the Communists to expand their influence. To Truman the invasion was part of the grand Communist scheme to destroy Western democracy and capitalism, a scheme that had begun with the Soviet takeover of Eastern Europe in 1945 and pro-Soviet factions' attempted takeover of Greece and Turkey in 1946. He had responded to the situation in the Mediterranean by proclaiming the Truman Doctrine, in which he declared that "it must be the policy of the United States to support free peoples who are resisting attempted subjugation by armed minorities or outside pressures." Supporting the South Koreans in their civil war against the North was a logical application of the Truman Doctrine.

The War Begins

In June 1950 the ROK had only ninety-eight thousand troops; since they were considered to be a constabulary rather than an army, they were equipped with small arms only, no tanks or artillery. In contrast, the NKPA was equipped with artillery and a brigade of Soviet-made tanks. The invasion caught the ROK by surprise, and within three days the NKPA had captured Seoul, the capital of South Korea. During the fighting for Seoul most of the ROK army was destroyed, putting the rest of South Korea in extreme jeopardy.

Two days after the invasion began Truman pledged military support for South Korea, and on July 1 the first U.S. troops arrived in Korea. The United States also persuaded the UN Security Council to condemn the invasion as a serious breach of world peace and call on UN member-nations to contribute troops to a multinational force to oust the NKPA. Normally the Soviet Union would have blocked such a move, but at the time the Soviet ambassador was boycotting council meetings to protest the award of China's seat on the council to tiny, pro-West Taiwan rather than Communist China. In short order, sixteen nations sent armed contingents to assist the South Koreans while a joint UN command, led by U.S. general Douglas MacArthur, was established. Nevertheless, most of the military force sent to support the ROK, including more than 90 percent of the air units, naval units, supplies, and money, was supplied by the United States.

Unawed by the military might arrayed against it, the NKPA pressed its attack. By the end of August it had captured all of South Korea except for a small area around Pusan, a major port in southeastern Korea, around which U.S./UN forces were able to maintain a defensive perimeter. But the NKPA had severely overextended itself, and on September 15 a significantly reinforced U.S./UN force outflanked the NKPA via a daring amphibious landing at Inchon, a major port just south of Seoul.

Caught off guard by the landing deep behind its lines, the NKPA was forced to retreat, and by October 1 it had abandoned most of the territory it had captured, including Seoul. Now on the offensive, U.S./UN troops (and a revived ROK army) crossed the 38th parallel, and by the end of October they had captured Pyongyang, the North Korean capital. The drive into North Korea continued all the way to the Yalu

River, the boundary between North Korea and Communist China.

The Chinese Enter the War

Up to this point Communist China had remained neutral. Despite its sympathy for the North Korean cause, so long as the Soviet-equipped NKPA was doing well, China was an observer. The presence of U.S./UN troops just across the Yalu, however, gave the Communist Chinese serious cause for concern. Mao Zedong, leader of the People's Republic of China, knew that the Americans, who supported Mao's archenemy Chiang Kai-shek, leader of the rival Republic of China on the island of Taiwan, would like nothing more than to overthrow his Communist regime and restore mainland China to Chiang. Fearing a two-pronged American-led invasion from Korea and Taiwan, Mao concluded that the Communist Chinese Forces (CCF) must expel the U.S./UN invaders from North Korea, and in early November the CCF engaged U.S. troops for the first time.

The CCF put more than 1 million well-equipped, well-trained men into the field against the U.S./UN forces, who soon found themselves outnumbered as much as ten to one. Once again the battle line crossed the 38th parallel as the CCF drove the U.S./UN forces back into South Korea and recaptured Seoul and Inchon. But another wave of reinforcements permitted the U.S./UN forces to counterattack in January 1951, and by the end of March the U.S./UN troops had retaken Seoul and Inchon. A CCF/NKPA counterattack in April was halted on the outskirts of Seoul, and shortly thereafter both sides took up positions along a line that ran more or less parallel to the 38th parallel.

An Armistice Ends the War

By June 1951 it had become apparent that neither side possessed the military muscle to evict the other from the Korean peninsula. Although fighting continued anyway, the conflict took on a rather desultory character. Consequently, on June 23 the Soviet Union called for armistice talks to begin, and on July 10 representatives from both sides met for talks at Kaesong, a city just south of the 38th parallel but behind North Korean lines. The talks broke off in August but were resumed in October at Panmunjom, a small village on the front line. They dragged on for a year with so little progress that in October 1952 the UN called for them to end. Meanwhile, both sides had solidified their defensive positions along the 38th parallel, and continued fighting devolved into skirmishes between small units rather than full-scale battles between large units.

By April 1953 it had become increasingly clear that neither side would be able to win a military victory. On April 26 armistice talks resumed, and this time both sides avoided protracted bickering. On July 27 an armistice was signed that recognized the line occupied by the respective sides as the boundary between North and South Korea. Ironically, this line ran more or less parallel to the 38th parallel, the boundary before the war, symbolizing for many the futility of a costly conflict.

The Cost of the War

The Korean War devastated Korea. Military and civilian casualties (dead, wounded, captured, and missing) totaled more than 2 million: Almost 50,000 South Koreans and more than 500,000 North Koreans died in the fighting or from the economic hardships that accompanied it. More than 33,600 American soldiers were killed and an estimated 900,000 Chinese soldiers were killed, wounded, or missing in action. All but two of Korea's major cities were damaged, many severely, while 43 percent of its industrial capacity and 33 percent of its homes were destroyed.

The financial costs were high as well. During the war the United Sates gave South Korea more than $12 million in military aid and more than $400 million in economic aid; much of the economic aid was used to purchase rice for impoverished Koreans whose crops were ravaged by the fighting. To help rebuild South Korea after the war the United Nations formed the Korean Reconstruction Agency, which raised and donated more than $148 million. In addition, the United States continued to pour financial aid into South Korea, a nominally democratic outpost in a Southeast Asia threatened by Communist takeovers during the next three decades, and by 1978 total American aid exceeded $5 billion. North Korea eschewed UN aid, preferring instead to accept assistance from the Soviet Union, China, and other Communist states or go it alone.

How the Korean War Affected Korea

The Korean War did little to change the country's political status quo: Korea remained divided into a pro-Communist North and a pro-Western, pro-capitalist South. Except for minor adjustments, even the boundary between North and South Korea remained essentially the same. However, the war did have important, drastically different economic and social consequences for the people of the two surviving Korean states.

In North Korea the repressive regime of Kim Il Sung became even more repressive as it remained committed, at least in theory, to its goal of reuniting Korea. Kim's long absolute dictatorship was characterized by a stagnant economy, dismal human rights record, massive poverty, rejection of Western influences, and secretive weapons development programs. Meanwhile, in South Korea a succession of regimes supported by massive U.S. aid shored up defenses against future northern aggression and embarked on ambitious, successful economic development programs.

The war resulted in important demographic changes in both Koreas. Rural Korea, already sparsely populated, became even more so as a result of the high casualty rate and the movement of people from the countryside to the cities in search of jobs and safety. North Korea was hit particularly hard, as an additional 2 million of its people fled to South Korea during and immediately after the war, thus further depleting its supply of labor for farms and factories.

The Korean War and the Course of the Cold War

From the beginning, American involvement in Korea had been justified as essential to stopping the spread of global communism. Although there was no clear victor in the Korean War, the U.S. government did claim a moral victory in that North Korea did not achieve unification and spread communism to the South. But the Communists of North Korea and the Soviet Union also claimed a victory of sorts, having driven U.S. and UN troops out of North Korea and kept them out, thus preserving Communist influence in the DPRK. The stalemate did nothing to reduce tensions between the two superpowers.

Perhaps the greatest legacy of the Korean War was that both Cold War antagonists now had a precedent for military intervention in Asia. Neither superpower was prepared to fight an unlimited nuclear war against its enemy, but both had now committed themselves to so-called proxy wars—backing and fighting conventional, limited wars in far-flung regional conflicts.

No sooner did the Korean War end than this commitment led the United States into Vietnam, another postcolonial Asian country erupting into civil war between Communist revolutionaries in the north and a pro-Western regime in the south. Again the USSR backed the northern Communists in this war of unification. There would be no permanent stalemate, however, in the Vietnam War, a twenty-year conflict that embittered and divided American society and that the United States ultimately lost. Though most Americans view Vietnam as the most important Cold War battlefield, it is the Korean War that provided the model, and its lessons are essential to understanding the Cold War.

LIVING THROUGH
THE COLD WAR

Speeches by World Leaders

Korea Must Be Reunified

Kim Il Sung

Kim Il Sung was the leader of the Democratic People's Republic of Korea (DPRK, or North Korea) when the Korean War broke out. Born in 1912, in the 1930s he became a Communist and a leader of armed resistance to the Japanese, who occupied Korea from 1909 to 1945. During World War II he served as a major in a Korean contingent of the Soviet Army and participated in the Soviet takeover of Korea from the Japanese north of the 38th parallel. In 1945, he became the leader of a pro-Soviet Communist government in the North. This government eventually became the DPRK, which Kim led until his death in 1994.

The primary objective of Kim's regime was the reunification of Korea under Korean self-rule. Having spent years working assiduously to oust Japanese troops and business interests from Korea, he devoted himself with equal fervor to ousting the United States from South Korea. Although he professed a desire to reunify Korea by peaceful means, in 1950 he set in motion a chain of events that culminated in the Korean War.

This viewpoint is taken from a speech Kim delivered in May 1950, just one month before he sent North Korean troops to invade the South. In it Kim accuses the United States of blocking the peaceful reunification of Korea, and it hints at the coming hostilities. The speech makes no secret of Kim's contempt for the United States and the pro-U.S. South Korean government of Syngman Rhee. Kim clearly sees the Soviets as the liberators of Korea and the Americans as greedy imperialists bent on turning Korea into their colony. To him, Americans are no different and no more welcome in Korea than the Japanese, who committed a number of atrocities against Koreans during their occupation.

Kim Il Sung, *For the Independent Peaceful Reunification of Korea.* New York: International, 1975.

Nearly five years have elapsed since our country was liberated from the protracted colonial oppression of Japanese imperialism and a broad avenue was opened up before our people for the building of a democratic and independent state. Korea is now a free country and for the first time the Korean people established their government on their land.

Immediately after liberation local people's committees were formed in all parts of Korea. The people's committees, formed with representatives of the workers, peasants, men in the cultural field, small tradesmen, entrepreneurs and people of various other strata, were a genuinely people's power. Under the leadership of the people's committees the Korean people set out on the building of democracy in their country.

But the Korean people's unanimous desire to develop their country into a unified independent and sovereign state has not been met.

U.S. Imperialism Prevents Korean Reunification

The aggressive army of U.S. imperialism entered south Korea one month after the Soviet troops had routed the Japanese army. As soon as the aggressive army of U.S. imperialism came, the reactionaries began to raise their heads in south Korea. Soon the Korean people clearly realized that the U.S. imperialists did not want Korea's independence but were plotting to make Korea their colony.

It was already evident right after liberation that north Korea where the Soviet army had come and south Korea where the U.S. army had entered were moving in opposite directions.

In August 1945 the Soviet army issued its first declaration to the Korean people. It reads in part:

> Korean people! . . . Korea has become a country of freedom.
> However, this marks only the first page in Korean history.
> An abundant, fruitful orchard is the result of man's efforts

and vigor. Therefore, the happiness of Korea, too, can only be achieved by the heroic efforts that you, the Korean people, will exert. Remember, Korean people! You have happiness in your own hands. You have attained liberty and liberation. Now everything is up to you. The Soviet army will provide the Korean people with all conditions for the free and creative labour you are bound to embark on. Koreans must make themselves the creators of their own happiness.

The Soviet army, as it had promised in this declaration, supported the people's committees in every way and provided all conditions for the Korean people to carry out democratic reforms and build a new happy life by their own hands.

In south Korea, however, the situation is totally different. The moment it arrived in south Korea, the U.S. army issued a proclamation in the name of [General Douglas] MacArthur [head of the U.S. Army's Far East Command], which read in part:

> All powers of government over the territory of Korea south of 38 degrees north latitude and the people thereof will be for the present exercised under my authority. Persons will obey my orders and orders issued under my authority. Acts of resistance to the occupying forces or any acts which may disturb public peace and safety will be punished severely.
>
> For all purposes during the military control, English will be the official language.

Carrying this proclamation into effect in south Korea, the U.S. military government authorities dissolved the people's committees which had been established by the people themselves according to their own will and deprived our people of their rights to speech, press, assembly and association, and imprisoned and murdered patriotic people. The U.S. imperialists pursued the reactionary policy of turning the southern half of our country into their colony.

When the U.S.S.R.-U.S. Joint Commission met to carry out the decision [to reunite Korea as a U.N. trust territory] of the Moscow three foreign ministers conference adopted in December 1945, the Soviet delegation made a determined effort for the establishment of a unified democratic government of Korea.

The U.S. imperialists, however, considered that if such a democratic united government should be established in Korea, their aggressive policy would be barred from being carried into reality. So, they stubbornly objected to the just Soviet proposal and torpedoed the decision of the Moscow conference.

The quisling [traitor] Syngman Rhee [president of South Korea] and other reactionary elements in Korea are despicable traitors who betrayed the interests of the country and the people; acting upon the U.S. military government's directive, they came out against the decision of the Moscow conference from the beginning under the slogan of "anti-trusteeship." They helped the U.S. imperialists to frustrate the implementation of the decision of the Moscow conference which fully conformed to the Korean people's interests and to wreck the work of the U.S.S.R.-U.S. Joint Commission.

Thus, Korea, freed from the Japanese occupationers' oppression, has been artificially divided with the 38th parallel as the demarcation line, and the south Korean people find themselves again groaning under the rule of the foreign invaders, the U.S. imperialists. . . .

U.S. Plans to Invade East Asia from South Korea

[The U.S. imperialists] are converting south Korea into a military base for invading the East and a supplier of raw materials and a market for the monopoly capitalists of Wall Street.

Early in 1948 they turned down the just proposal put forward by the Government of the Soviet Union on simultaneously withdrawing the troops of the Soviet Union and the

United States from Korea and leaving the solution of the Korean question to the Korean people themselves.

They unlawfully brought the Korean question to the UN General Assembly, fabricated the "UN Commission on Korea" by using their voting machine and, assisted by this commission, held a separate election in south Korea on May 10, 1948.

All the patriotic political parties, social organizations and people of Korea put up a stubborn struggle in opposition to the holding of a separate election in south Korea and the establishment of a separate puppet government.

A joint conference of representatives of political parties and social organizations of north and south Korea was held in April 1948 at the proposal of the Workers' Party. The conference was attended by representatives of 56 right, left and middle-of-the-road political parties and social organizations embracing over 10 million members. Only traitors like Syngman Rhee refused to participate in it.

The April north-south joint conference fully exposed the "UN Commission on Korea" as a tool for executing the U.S. imperialists' policy of colonial plunder. It decided on rejecting the separate election to be held in south Korea on May 10 and declared that the Korean people would not recognize a government, which would be established through this separate election, ruinous to the nation. Such a government could in no way represent the Korean people.

The South Korean Assembly Does Not Represent the People

However, the south Korean reactionary clique and the U.S. imperialists held a separate election in south Korea by force of arms, terrorism and blackmailing and concocted a reactionary Syngman Rhee puppet government composed of traitors to the nation, the former lackeys of Japanese imperialism and the stooges of U.S. imperialism.

Among the so-called "members of the National Assembly" there is not a single representative of the workers or the peasants who are the overwhelming majority of the Korean people. This alone is enough to show the anti-popular nature of the reactionary puppet regime.

The establishment of a puppet regime through the separate election in south Korea is a trickery of the U.S. imperialists and their lackeys to perpetuate the artificial division of Korea. That is why the leaders of some 30 patriotic political parties and social organizations in north and south Korea held another conference in June 1948 and declared the separate election illegal and, at the same time, decided on holding a general election throughout north and south Korea, founding a unified Democratic People's Republic of Korea and establishing a democratic central government.

The general election to the Supreme People's Assembly of Korea was held throughout north and south Korea on August 25, 1948. Although the pro-Japanese elements and traitors to the nation, relying on the arms of the U.S. imperialists, resorted to harsh repression and terrorism, 77.52 percent of the electors participated in the election in the southern half. In the north where the election was held in a free atmosphere, 99.97 percent of the electors went to the polls.

As you see, the Supreme People's Assembly is the supreme legislative body of Korea which has been established through an all-Korea election. The First Session of the Supreme People's Assembly proclaimed our country to be the Democratic People's Republic of Korea, adopted the Constitution and set up the Government of the D.P.R.K.

The Constitution of the D.P.R.K. confirmed by law the successes of all the democratic reforms carried out in the northern half of our country, granted true democratic rights to the working people and opened up broad vistas for founding a unified democratic state. The Constitution expresses the centuries-old desire of our people.

The Government of the Republic, which was approved at the First Session of the Supreme People's Assembly of Korea, was of a coalition cabinet, and it embraced representatives of major political parties and social organizations of north and south Korea. Thus, the Government of the D.P.R.K. which has been formed as a result of the general election is the only legal government in Korea and enjoys the support of the entire Korean people.

At the request of the First Session of the Supreme People's Assembly of Korea, the Soviet government has withdrawn its troops from our territory, recognized the D.P.R.K. and established diplomatic relations with our country.

The founding of the D.P.R.K. marked a new stage in the struggle of our people to build a unified independent country. All the patriotic political parties, social organizations and popular masses of Korea, firmly rallied around the Government of the People's Republic, are struggling with increasing stamina to consolidate the political and economic base of the Republic and promote national reunification.

The heroic people of south Korea are stepping up a powerful all-people struggle to overthrow the Syngman Rhee puppet regime which the U.S. imperialists and their stooges have rigged up against the will of the people.

North and South Korea Are Becoming Increasingly Different

North and south Korea are going different ways. As the days go by, the sharp contrast between the political and economic situations in north and south Korea shows more convincingly which is the right path leading the country and the people to prosperity.

The U.S. troops keep staying in south Korea even now when the Soviet troops have withdrawn from north Korea. The U.S. imperialists have concluded the "ROK [Republic of Korea, or South Korea]-U.S. Agreement on Military Assistance" and the "ROK-U.S. Agreement on Economic Assistance" with the anti-popular puppet regime and have converted the southern half of our country into their colony.

The southern half of our country ruled by the traitorous Syngman Rhee clique has been transformed into a land of darkness where reactionary terrorism and violent repression prevail.

Under the patronage of U.S. imperialists and their agent, the "UN Commission on Korea," the treacherous Syngman Rhee clique is harshly suppressing not only the left forces but also the right elements who are discontented with their reactionary rule. The Syngman Rhee police have arrested and imprisoned 12 "national assemblymen" in violation of the law which provides for their "inviolability."

Syngman Rhee murdered Kim Gu, a right-wing leader, simply because the latter had advocated the peaceful reunification of the country. The Syngman Rhee clique is slaughtering progressive men in the field of culture for not making statements in support of the puppet government.

Backed up by the bayonets of the U.S. imperialists, this clique is trying desperately to maintain its rule in south Korea by means of suppression, terrorism and massacre, and is even going to such length as destroying people en masse.

The appalling situation in south Korea brought about by the reactionary rule of the U.S. imperialists and the Syngman Rhee clique, their stooge, is calling forth the indignation and strong resistance of the working masses.

An extensive guerrilla struggle of the people is now underway throughout south Korea to oppose the colonial policy of the U.S. imperialists and overthrow Syngman Rhee's reactionary ruling system.

In this situation, an urgent need arose for all the patriotic political parties and social organizations of our country to take new measures to struggle for territorial integrity and national reunification.

With a view to rallying all the patriotic democratic forces in a more vigorous struggle against reaction, we organized the Democratic Front for the Reunification of the Fatherland late in June 1949, which embraced 71 political parties and social organizations of north and south Korea.

The inaugural meeting of the Democratic Front for the Reunification of the Fatherland discussed the situation in our country and put forward a proposal for attaining peaceful reunification in order to liberate the people in the southern half who are groaning under the terrorist rule of the Syngman Rhee puppet regime, foil the scheme of the Syngman Rhee clique to launch a fratricidal war at the instigation of the U.S. imperialists, and save the country and the people.

The justness of this proposal is clear for all to see. In its proposal, the Democratic Front for the Reunification of the Fatherland demanded the immediate withdrawal of the U.S. troops from south Korea and the "UN Commission on Korea," a tool serving the aggressive ends of the U.S. imperialists, and the guaranteeing of lawfulness for the democratic political parties and social organizations and their freedom of activities. It demanded a general election throughout north and south Korea free from foreign interference, peaceful reunification of Korea, and the entire Korean people's choice of a state system of their own free will.

North Korea Supports Peaceful Reunification

This proposal on peaceful reunification won enthusiastic support from the entire Korean people. But it did not agree in the least with the aggressive and anti-popular aims of the U.S. imperialists and the reactionaries, their lackeys, who were pursuing a colonial enslavement policy in south Korea. The Syngman Rhee clique could not accept this proposal because they were aware that they could maintain their rule only under the patronage of the U.S. armed forces. By turning down this proposal, they showed ever more clearly that they were afraid of the Korean people and betrayed their true colors as traitors to the Korean people.

The Korean people have risen in the struggle to overthrow the Syngman Rhee puppet regime that is obstructing the peaceful reunification of the country. This greatly alarms the U.S. imperialists. The U.S. imperialists have instigated the Syngman Rhee clique to launch frequent armed clashes along the 38th parallel in order to find a pretext to interfere in the internal affairs of Korea. At the same time, by using their voting machine, they have resorted to such underhand manoeuvres as to illegally place the Korean question again on the agenda of the fourth session of the UN General Assembly and dispatch the third "UN Commission on Korea."

The Korean people are well aware of the aims of the "UN Commission on Korea."

The first "UN Commission on Korea," a tool of the U.S. imperialists in carrying out their colonial enslavement policy in Korea, was sent to our country to legalize the separate election in south Korea and the establishment of the Syngman Rhee puppet regime. The mission of the second "UN Commission on Korea" was to justify the Syngman Rhee puppet regime terrorizing and massacring the people under the manipulation of the U.S. imperialists. And the third "UN Commission on Korea" is scheming to save the Syngman Rhee puppet regime from ruin and make Korea a permanent colony of U.S. imperialists.

Recently, with the start of the aggressive acts by the new "U.N. Commission on Korea," the traitorous Syngman Rhee clique is fussing about introducing a "UN police force" into south Korea under the manipulation of the U.S. imperialists and is even preparing for the formation of an alliance with the Japanese imperialists.

However, no aggressive intrigue of the U.S. imperialists will ever be realized. The Korean people do not want uninvited guests who are encroaching upon the independence and freedom of their country.

The U.S. imperialists must clearly see that the Korean people today are different from what they were yesterday.

Our people are not a flock of sheep who allow a pack of wolves to eat them up.

North Korea Supports Happiness, Freedom, and Democracy

Today the Korean people have their fatherland, the Democratic People's Republic of Korea, and a powerful political and economic base. In the course of building democracy in the northern half of the Republic over the five years since liberation, our people have personally experienced true freedom and happiness as a people in power. The Korean people, who have been freed from 36 years of colonial oppression by Japanese imperialism, will not yield to anyone the rights and freedom they have won and will not become colonial slaves again. The Korean people will never allow the U.S. imperialists to subjugate and plunder their country.

Our people are now in a struggle to implement the proposal of the Democratic Front for the Reunification of the Fatherland on the country's peaceful reunification in order to attain complete national independence, develop the country along democratic lines and win peaceful reunification. A graphic illustration of this struggle can be seen in the fact that the people in the northern half of the Republic are energetically building democracy to strengthen the political and economic base of our Republic and that the people in the southern half are putting up a mass resistance and ever-growing guerrilla struggle against the U.S. imperialists and the Syngman Rhee traitorous clique, their lackeys.

The Korean people are by no means alone in their just struggle to win their country's complete freedom and independence. All the peoples of the world who love peace and democracy are supporting our struggle.

The Workers' Party, the Democratic Front for the Reunification of the Fatherland led by the Party, the Government of the D.P.R.K. and all the Korean people who are rallied around it, will advance vigorously for the complete independence and reunification of their country and for peace and democracy. They will certainly win the final victory.

Americans Should Support the War Effort in Korea

Harry S. Truman

Harry S. Truman was the president of the United States when the Korean War broke out. Born in 1884, Truman served in the U.S. Senate and as vice president before taking office following the death of President Franklin D. Roosevelt in 1945. Elected to a term in his own right in 1948, he returned to private life in 1953, about six months before an armistice brought the fighting in Korea to an end.

Unlike Roosevelt, Truman felt uncomfortable working with the Soviets, who had been American allies during World War II. Truman took seriously the pronouncements of former Soviet leader Vladimir I. Lenin, who had committed the Soviet Union to work for the global spread of communism. In 1947 Truman issued a foreign policy statement known as the Truman Doctrine, which pledged U.S. support for Greece and Turkey against the apparent threat of takeovers by pro-Soviet Communists. Truman's other anti-Soviet initiatives included the Marshall Plan of 1948, which pledged billions of U.S. dollars for rebuilding war-torn Europe, thus safeguarding it from Communist expansion, and the North Atlantic Treaty Organization (NATO) pact of 1949, by which the nations of Western Europe and North America committed themselves to defend each other against Communist aggression. In fact, after World War II the primary focus of the Truman administration was to combat the spread of communism.

This viewpoint is taken from the president's radio and television address to the nation on the evening of July 19, 1950. Truman outlines his reasons for committing U.S. troops to fight in Korea, clearly indicating his view of the invasion of South Korea

Harry S. Truman, radio and television address to the American people, Washington, DC, July 19, 1950.

not as an attempt to reunify that country under Korean rule but as part of the Communists' grand strategy to take over the world. The speech also calls on Americans to do their part in support of the war effort, such as pay higher taxes and refuse to profiteer in or hoard scarce goods.

My fellow citizens:

At noon today I sent a message to the Congress about the situation in Korea. I want to talk to you tonight about that situation, and about what it means to the security of the United States and to our hopes for peace in the world.

Korea is a small country, thousands of miles away, but what is happening there is important to every American.

On Sunday, June 25th, Communist forces attacked the Republic of Korea.

This attack has made it clear, beyond all doubt, that the international Communist movement is willing to use armed invasion to conquer independent nations. An act of aggression such as this creates a very real danger to the security of all free nations.

The attack upon Korea was an outright breach of the peace and a violation of the Charter of the United Nations. By their actions in Korea, Communist leaders have demonstrated their contempt for the basic moral principles on which the United Nations is founded. This is a direct challenge to the efforts of the free nations to build the kind of world in which men can live in freedom and peace.

This challenge has been presented squarely. We must meet it squarely.

The Facts About Korea

It is important for all of us to understand the essential facts as to how the situation in Korea came about.

Before and during World War II, Korea was subject to Japanese rule. When the fighting stopped, it was agreed that troops of the Soviet Union would accept the surrender of the Japanese soldiers in the northern part of Korea, and that American forces would accept the surrender of the Japanese in the southern part. For this purpose, the 38th parallel was used as the dividing line.

Later, the United Nations sought to establish Korea as a free and independent nation. A commission was sent out to supervise a free election in the whole of Korea. However, this election was held only in the southern part of the country, because the Soviet Union refused to permit an election for this purpose to be held in the northern part. Indeed, the Soviet authorities even refused to permit the United Nations Commission to visit northern Korea.

Nevertheless, the United Nations decided to go ahead where it could. In August 1948 the Republic of Korea was established as a free and independent nation in that part of Korea south of the 38th parallel.

In December 1948, the Soviet Union stated that it had withdrawn its troops from northern Korea and that a local government had been established there. However, the Communist authorities never have permitted the United Nations observers to visit northern Korea to see what was going on behind that part of the Iron Curtain.

It was from that area, where the Communist authorities have been unwilling to let the outside world see what was going on, that the attack was launched against the Republic of Korea on June 25th. That attack came without provocation and without warning. It was an act of raw aggression, without a shadow of justification.

I repeat that it was an act of raw aggression. It had no justification whatever.

The Communist invasion was launched in great force, with planes, tanks, and artillery. The size of the attack, and the speed with which it was followed up, make it perfectly plain that it had been plotted long in advance.

Asking the United Nations for Help

As soon as word of the attack was received, Secretary of State [Dean] Acheson called me at Independence, Mo., and informed me that, with my approval, he would ask for an immediate meeting of the United Nations Security Council. The Security Council met just 24 hours after the Communist invasion began.

One of the main reasons the Security Council was set up was to act in such cases as this—to stop outbreaks of aggression in a hurry before they develop into general conflicts. In this case the Council passed a resolution which called for the invaders of Korea to stop fighting, and to withdraw. The Council called on all members of the United Nations to help carry out this resolution. The Communist invaders ignored the action of the Security Council and kept right on with their attack.

The Security Council then met again. It recommended that members of the United Nations help the Republic of Korea repel the attack and help restore peace and security in that area.

Fifty-two of the 59 countries which are members of the United Nations have given their support to the action taken by the Security Council to restore peace in Korea.

These actions by the United Nations and its members are of great importance. The free nations have now made it clear that lawless aggression will be met with force. The free nations have learned the fateful lesson of the 1930's. That lesson is that aggression must be met firmly. Appeasement leads only to further aggression and ultimately to war.

The principal effort to help the Koreans preserve their independence, and to help the United Nations restore peace, has been made by the United States. We have sent land, sea, and air forces to assist in these operations. We have done this because we know that what is at stake here is nothing less than our own national security and the peace of the world.

So far, two other nations—Australia and Great Britain—have sent planes to Korea; and six other nations—Australia, Canada, France, Great Britain, the Netherlands, and New Zealand—have made naval forces available.

Under the flag of the United Nations a unified command has been established for all forces of the members of the United Nations fighting in Korea. Gen. Douglas MacArthur is the commander of this combined force.

The prompt action of the United Nations to put down lawless aggression, and the prompt response to this action by free peoples all over the world, will stand as a landmark in mankind's long search for a rule of law among nations.

Soviets Refuse to Act

Only a few countries have failed to endorse the efforts of the United Nations to stop the fighting in Korea. The most important of these is the Soviet Union. The Soviet Union has boycotted the meetings of the United Nations Security Council. It has refused to support the actions of the United Nations with respect to Korea.

The United States requested the Soviet Government, 2 days after the fighting started, to use its influence with the North Koreans to have them withdraw. The Soviet Government refused.

The Soviet Government has said many times that it wants peace in the world, but its attitude toward this act of aggression against the Republic of Korea is in direct contradiction of its statements.

For our part, we shall continue to support the United Nations action to restore peace in the world.

We know that it will take a hard, tough fight to halt the invasion, and to drive the Communists back. The invaders have been provided with enough equipment and supplies for a long campaign. They overwhelmed the lightly armed defense forces of the Korean Republic in the first few days and drove southward.

Now, however, the Korean defenders have reorganized and are making a brave fight for their liberty, and an increasing number of American troops have joined them. Our forces have fought a skillful, rearguard delaying action, pending the arrival of reinforcements. Some of these reinforcements are now arriving; others are on the way from the United States.

Americans Are Putting Up a Good Fight

I should like to read you a part of a report I have received from General [Joseph] Collins, Chief of Staff of the United States Army. General Collins and General [Hoyt] Vandenberg, Chief of Staff of the Air Force, have just returned from an inspection trip to Korea and Japan. This is what General Collins had to say:

> The United States Armed Forces in Korea are giving a splendid account of themselves.
>
> Our Far Eastern forces were organized and equipped primarily to perform peaceful occupation duties in Japan. However, under General MacArthur's magnificent leadership, they have quickly adapted themselves to meet the deliberately planned attack of the North Korean Communist forces, which are well-equipped, well-led, and battle-trained, and which have at times outnumbered our troops by as much as 20 to 1.
>
> Our Army troops, ably supported by tactical aircraft of the United States Air Force and Navy and our Australian friends, flying under the most adverse conditions of weather, have already distinguished themselves in the most difficult of military operations—a delaying action. The fact that they are preventing the Communists from overrunning Korea—which this calculated attack had been designed to accom-

plish—is a splendid tribute to the ability of our Armed Forces to convert quickly from the peaceful duties of occupation to the grim duties of war.

The task that confronts us is not an easy one, but I am confident of the outcome.

I shall also read to you part of a report that I received from General MacArthur within the last few hours. General MacArthur says:

It is, of course, impossible to predict with any degree of accuracy the future incidents of a military campaign. Over a broad front involving continuous local struggles, there are bound to be ups and downs, losses as well as successes. . . . But the issue of battle is now fully joined and will proceed along lines of action in which we will not be without choice. Our hold upon the southern part of Korea represents a secure base. Our casualties, despite overwhelming odds, have been relatively light. Our strength will continually increase while that of the enemy will relatively decrease. His supply line is insecure. He has had his great chance and failed to exploit it. We are now in Korea in force, and with God's help we are there to stay until the constitutional authority of the Republic of Korea is fully restored.

These and other reports I have received show that our Armed Forces are acting with close teamwork and efficiency to meet the problems facing us in Korea.

These reports are reassuring, but they also show that the job ahead of us in Korea is long and difficult.

Furthermore, the fact that Communist forces have invaded Korea is a warning that there may be similar acts of aggression in other parts of the world. The free nations must be on their guard more than ever before, against this kind of sneak attack.

Troops, Money, and Supplies

It is obvious that we must increase our military strength and preparedness immediately. There are three things we need to do.

First, we need to send more men, equipment, and supplies to General MacArthur.

Second, in view of the world situation, we need to build up our own Army, Navy, and Air Force over and above what is needed in Korea.

Third, we need to speed up our work with other countries in strengthening our common defenses.

To help meet these needs, I have already authorized increases in the size of our Armed Forces. These increases will come in part from volunteers, in part from Selective Service, and in part from the National Guard and the Reserves.

I have also ordered that military supplies and equipment be obtained at a faster rate.

The necessary increases in the size of our Armed Forces, and the additional equipment they must have, will cost about $10 billion, and I am asking the Congress to appropriate the amount required.

These funds will be used to train men and equip them with tanks, planes, guns, and ships, in order to build the strength we need to help assure peace in the world.

When we have worked out with other free countries an increased program for our common defense, I shall recommend to the Congress that additional funds be provided for this purpose. This is of great importance. The free nations face a worldwide threat. It must be met with a worldwide defense. The United States and other free nations can multiply their strength by joining with one another in a common effort to provide this defense. This is our best hope for peace.

The things we need to do to build up our military defense will require considerable adjustment in our domestic economy.

We have a tremendously rich and productive economy, and it is expanding every year.

Our job now is to divert to defense purposes more of that tremendous productive capacity—more steel, more aluminum, more of a good many things.

Some of the additional production for military purposes can come from making fuller use of plants which are not operating at capacity. But many of our industries are already going full tilt, and until we can add new capacity, some of the resources we need for the national defense will have to be taken from civilian uses.

This requires us to take certain steps to make sure that we obtain the things we need for national defense, and at the same time guard against inflationary price rises.

The steps that are needed now must be taken promptly.

In the message which I sent to the Congress today, I described the economic measures which are required at this time.

First, we need laws which will insure prompt and adequate supplies for military and essential civilian use. I have therefore recommended that the Congress give the Government power to guide the flow of materials into essential uses, to restrict their use for nonessential purposes, and to prevent the accumulation of unnecessary inventories.

Second, we must adopt measures to prevent inflation and to keep our Government in a sound financial condition. One of the major causes of inflation is the excessive use of credit. I have recommended that the Congress authorize the Government to set limits on installment buying and to curb speculation in agricultural commodities. In the housing field, where Government credit is an important factor, I have already directed that credit restraints be applied, and I have recommended that the Congress authorize further controls.

As an additional safeguard against inflation, and to help finance our defense needs, it will be necessary to make substantial increases in taxes. This is a contribution to our national security that every one of us should stand ready to make. As soon as a balanced and fair tax program can be worked out, I shall lay it before the Congress. This tax program will have as a major aim the elimination of profiteering.

Third, we should increase the production of goods needed for national defense. We must plan to enlarge our defense production, not just for the immediate future, but for the next several years. This will be primarily a task for our businessmen and workers. However, to help obtain the necessary increases, the Government should be authorized to provide certain types of financial assistance to private industry to increase defense production.

Civilians Must Do Their Part

Our military needs are large, and to meet them will require hard work and steady effort. I know that we can produce what we need if each of us does his part—each man, each woman, each soldier, each civilian. This is a time for all of us to pitch in and work together.

I have been sorry to hear that some people have fallen victim to rumors in the last week or two, and have been buying up various things they have heard would be scarce. That is foolish—I say that is foolish, and it is selfish, very selfish, because hoarding results in entirely unnecessary local shortages.

Hoarding food is especially foolish. There is plenty of food in this country. I have read that there have been runs on sugar in some cities. That is perfectly ridiculous. We now have more sugar available than ever before. There are ample supplies of our other basic foods also.

Now, I sincerely hope that every American housewife will keep this in mind when she does her daily shopping.

If I had thought that we were actually threatened by shortages of essential consumer goods, I should have recommended that price control and rationing be immediately instituted. But there is no such threat. We have to fear only those shortages which we ourselves artificially create.

Every businessman who is trying to profiteer in time of national danger—and every person who is selfishly trying to get more than his neighbor—is doing just exactly the thing that any enemy of this country would want him to do.

If prices should rise unduly because of excessive buying or speculation, I know our people will want the Government to take action, and I will not hesitate to recommend rationing and price control.

We have the resources to meet our needs. Far more important, the American people are unified in their belief in democratic freedom. We are united in detesting Communist slavery.

We know that the cost of freedom is high. But we are determined to preserve our freedom—no matter what the cost.

I know that our people are willing to do their part to support our soldiers and sailors and airmen who are fighting in Korea. I know that our fighting men can count on each and every one of you.

Our country stands before the world as an example of how free men, under God, can build a community of neighbors, working together for the good of all.

That is the goal we seek not only for ourselves, but for all people. We believe that freedom and peace are essential if men are to live as our Creator intended us to live. It is this faith that has guided us in the past, and it is this faith that will fortify us in the stern days ahead.

The United States Should Get Out of Korea

Herbert Hoover

Not all Americans agreed with President Harry S. Truman that the spread of communism must be stopped, with military force if necessary. Many Americans, including leading fiscal conservatives, preferred to follow a program that has come to be called "Fortress America." Its proponents believed that a North America with adequate naval and air defenses would be so impregnable that the United States would not need the help of allies in Europe or Asia to keep its shores safe from a Communist invasion. Fortress America was inspired in large part by the brilliant showing of the British during World War II; Great Britain possessed few tanks or ground troops, but its navy and air force staved off a German invasion even as Hitler's armies rolled over the rest of Europe. Fortress America's proponents called for the United States to build up its navy and air force to be the best in the world while minimizing ground troop forces. They also called for a foreign policy that included formal refusal to involve the United States in foreign ground wars that would only wear down the military and drain the economy.

Herbert Hoover, Republican president of the United States from 1929 to 1933, was a fiscal conservative who had opposed government intervention as a means of alleviating the worst effects of the Great Depression. Hoover was trounced in his 1932 bid for reelection by Democrat Franklin D. Roosevelt, whose New Deal and four-term presidency vastly increased the size and scope of the federal government. But Hoover returned to government service from 1947 to 1949 to chair a federal commission on the elimination of waste in government. This selection is taken from a radio address Hoover gave on December 20, 1950, about three weeks after the Communist Chinese entered the Korean

Herbert Hoover, *Address Upon the American Road, 1950–1955*. Stanford, CA: Stanford University Press, 1955.

War. At the time, U.S. troops were retreating before the vastly superior numbers of the Chinese, and it looked as if the Americans could not possibly win the war, with or without greater assistance from the United Nations. In the speech, Hoover calls on the United States to commit itself to the fight against communism via the Fortress America program, not Truman's containment policy.

I have received hundreds of requests that I appraise the present situation and give my conclusions as to our national policies.

I speak with a deep sense of responsibility. And I speak tonight under the anxieties of every American for the nation's sons who are fighting and dying on a mission of peace and the honor of our country.

No appraisal of the world situation can be final in an unstable world. However, to find our national path we must constantly reexamine where we have arrived and at times revise our direction. I do not propose to traverse the disastrous road by which we reached this point.

The Global Situation

We may first survey the global military situation. There is today only one center of aggression on the earth. That is the Communist-controlled Asian-European land mass of 800 million people. They have probably over 300 trained and equipped combat divisions with over 30,000 tanks, 10,000 tactical planes, and further large reserves they can put in action in ninety days. But they are not a great sea power. Their long-range air power is limited. This congeries of over thirty different races will some day go to pieces. But in the meantime they furnish unlimited cannon fodder.

Facing this menace on the Eastern front there are about 100 million non-Communist island people in Japan, Formosa [Taiwan], the Philippines, and Korea. Aside from Korea . . .

they have probably only twelve effective combat divisions with practically no tanks, air, or navy.

Facing this land mass on the south are the [East] Indies and the Middle East of about 600 million non-Communist people. There are about 150 million further non-Communist people in North Africa and Latin America. Except Turkey and Formosa, these 850 million non-Communist people have little military force which they would or could spare. But they could contribute vital economic and moral strength.

Facing this menace on the Continental European front there are about 160 million further non-Communist people who, excluding Spain, have less than twenty combat divisions now available, few tanks, and little air or naval force. And their will to defend themselves is feeble and their disunities are manifest.

Of importance in military weight at this moment there is the British Commonwealth of 150 million people, with probably thirty combat divisions under arms, a superior Navy, considerable Air Force, and a few tanks.

And there are 150 million people in the United States preparing 3.5 million men into a gigantic Air Force and Navy, with about thirty equipped combat divisions.

Thus there are 1,310,000,000 non-Communist people in the world, of whom today only about 320 million have any military potency.

Facing the Facts

If we weigh these military forces as they stand today, we must arrive at certain basic conclusions:

1. We must face the fact that to commit the sparse ground forces of the non-Communist nations into a land war against this Communist land mass would be a war without victory, a war without a successful political terminal. The Germans failed with a magnificent army of 240 combat divisions and with powerful air and tank forces.

That compares with only 60 divisions proposed today for the North Atlantic Pact nations. Even were Western Europe armed far beyond any contemplated program, we could never reach Moscow. Therefore, any attempt to make war on the Communist mass by land invasion, through the quicksands of China, India, or Western Europe, is sheer folly. That would be the graveyard of millions of American boys and would end in the exhaustion of this Gibraltar of Western civilization.

2. Equally, we Americans alone, with sea and air power, can so control the Atlantic and Pacific Oceans that there can be no possible invasion of the Western Hemisphere by Communist armies. They can no more reach Washington in force than we can reach Moscow.

3. In this military connection we must realize the fact that the atomic bomb is a far less dominant weapon than it was once thought to be.

4. It is obvious that the United Nations have been defeated in Korea by the aggression of Communist China. There are no available forces in the world to repel them. Even if we sacrifice more American boys to hold a bridgehead, we know we shall not succeed at the present time in the mission given to us by the fifty members of the United Nations.

We may explore our American situation still further. The 150 million American people are already economically strained by government expenditures. It must not be forgotten that we are carrying huge burdens from previous wars, including obligations to veterans and $260 billion of bond and currency issues from those wars. In the fiscal year 1952, federal and local expenditures are likely to exceed $90 billion. That is more than our total savings. We must finance huge deficits by further government issues. Inflation is already moving. The dollar has in six months fallen 15 or 20 percent in purchasing power. But we might with stern measures avoid the economic disintegration of such a load for a very few years. If we continued long on this road, the one center of resistance in the world will collapse in economic disaster.

The Diplomatic Situation

We may also appraise the diplomatic front. Our great hope was in the United Nations. We have witnessed the sabotage of its primary purpose of preserving peace. It has been . . . a forum for continuous smear on our honor, our ideals, and our purposes. It did stiffen up against raw aggression last July in Korea. But in its call for that military action, America had to furnish over 90 percent of the foreign forces and suffer over 90 percent of their dead and injured. That effort now comes at least to a measurable military defeat by the aggression of Communist hordes.

Whether or not the United Nations is to have a moral defeat and suffer the collapse of its whole moral stature now depends on whether it has the courage to:

1. Declare Communist China an aggressor.

2. Refuse admission of this aggressor to its membership.

3. Demand that each member of the United Nations cease to furnish or transport supplies of any kind to Communist China that can aid in their military operations. Such a course honestly carried out by the non-Communist nations is not economic sanctions nor does it require military actions. But it would constitute a great pressure for rectitude.

4. For once, pass a resolution condemning the infamous lies about the United States.

Any course short of such action is appeasement.

Where We Should Go from Here

And now I come to where we should go from here. . . .

First, the foundation of our national policies must be to preserve for the world this Western Hemisphere Gibraltar of Western civilization.

Second, we can, without any measure of doubt, with our own air and naval forces, hold the Atlantic and Pacific Oceans with one frontier on Britain (if she wishes to cooperate); the other, on Japan, Formosa, and the Philippines. We can hold open the sea lanes for our supplies. And I devoutly hope that a maximum of cooperation can be established between the British Commonwealth and ourselves.

Third, to do this we should arm our air and naval forces to the teeth. We have little need for large armies unless we are going to Europe or China. We should give Japan her independence and aid her in arms to defend herself. We should stiffen the defenses of our Pacific frontier in Formosa and the Philippines. We can protect this island chain by our sea and air power.

Fourth, we could, after initial outlays for more air and navy equipment, greatly reduce our expenditures, balance our budget, and free ourselves from the dangers of inflation and economic degeneration.

Fifth, if we toil and sacrifice as the President has so well asked, we can continue aid to the hungry of the world. Out of our productivity, we can give aid to other nations when they have already displayed spirit and strength in defense against Communism. We have the stern duty to work and sacrifice to do it.

Sixth, we should have none of appeasement. Morally there is no appeasement of Communism. Appeasement contains more dangers than Dunkirks [a World War II triumph of morale in the face of certain disaster]. We want no more Teherans and no more Yaltas [sites of treaties that supposedly favored the Soviets over the Americans and British]. We can retrieve a battle but we cannot retrieve an appeasement. We are grateful that President Truman has denounced such a course.

Seventh, we are not blind to the need to preserve Western civilization on the continent of Europe or to our cultural and religious ties to it. But the prime obligation of defense of Western Continental Europe rests upon the nations of Europe. The test is whether they have the spiritual force, the will, and acceptance of unity among them by their own volition. America cannot create their spiritual forces; we cannot buy them with money.

Europeans Are Confused

You can search all the history of mankind and there is no parallel to the effort and sacrifice we have made to elevate their spirit and to achieve their unity. To this date it has failed. Their minds are confused with fears and disunities. They exclude Spain, although she has the will and means to fight. They higgle with Germany, although she is their frontier. They vacillate in the belief that they are in little danger and they hope to avoid again being a theater of war. And Karl Marx has added to their confusions. They still suffer from battle shock. Their highly organized Communist parties are a menace that we must not ignore.

In both World War I and World War II (including West Germany) those nations placed more than 250 trained and equipped combat divisions in the field within sixty days, with strong air and naval forces. They have more manpower and more productive capacity today than in either one of those wars. To warrant our further aid they should show they have spiritual strength and unity to avail themselves of their own resources. But it must be far more than pacts, conferences, paper promises, and declarations. Today it must express itself in organized and equipped combat divisions of such huge numbers as would erect a sure dam against the red [Communist] flood. And that before we land another man or another dollar on their shores. Otherwise we shall be inviting another Korea. That would be a calamity to Europe as well as to us. Our policy in this quarter of the world should be confined to a period of watchful waiting before we take on any commitments.

There is a proper urge in all Americans for unity in troubled times. But unless unity is based on right principles and right action it is a vain and dangerous thing. Honest difference of views and honest debate are not disunity. They are the vital process of policymaking among free men.

A right, a specific, an open foreign policy must be formulated which gives confidence in our own security before we can get behind it.

American eyes should now be opened to these hordes in Asia.

Avoiding Rash Involvements

These policies I have suggested would be no isolationism. Indeed, they are the opposite. They would avoid rash involvement of our military forces in hopeless campaigns. They do not relieve us of working to our utmost. They would preserve a stronghold of Christian civilization in the world against any peradventure.

With the policies I have outlined, even without Europe, Americans have no reason for hysteria or loss of confidence in our security or our future. And in American security rests the future security of all mankind.

It would be an uneasy peace, but we could carry it on with these policies indefinitely even if the Communists should attack our lines on the seas.

We can hope that in time the more than a billion of other non-Communist peoples of the world will rise to their dangers. We can hope that sometime the evils of Communism and the crumbling of their racial controls will bring their own disintegration. It is a remote consolation, but twice before in world history Asiatic hordes [the Huns and Mongols] have swept over a large part of the world and their racial dissensions dissolved their empires.

Our people have braved difficult and distressing situations in these three centuries we have been on this continent. We have faced our troubles without fear and we have not failed. We shall not fail in this, even if we have to stand alone. But we need to realize the whole truth and gird ourselves for troubled times. The truth is ugly. We face it with prayer and courage. The Almighty is on our side.

LIVING THROUGH
THE COLD WAR

CHAPTER 2

I U.S. Soldiers in the War

A Reservist Goes Off to War

William B. Hopkins

When the Korean War broke out in 1950, the U.S. military was woefully unprepared. In the general decommissioning that followed the end of World War II, troop strength had been reduced in the Far East to a mere four divisions, most of whom were enjoying occupation duty in Japan. The federal government quickly moved to increase its military strength by calling to active duty more than a quarter-million reservists. Although many of these men and women had served in World War II, most had joined the Reserves expecting to earn some extra money in civilian life or, in any event, perform Cold War military service that stopped short of armed conflict. Nevertheless, reservists fought bravely in Korea, where they won seven Medals of Honor, five of them posthumously. They were also sorely missed at home by their families, friends, clients, and employers, and their departure for Korea left a void in their communities.

William B. Hopkins commanded Headquarters and Service (H&S) Company, First Battalion, First Marine Division during the Korean War. He had served with the Marine Corps (USMC) in the South Pacific during World War II, taken up the practice of law in Roanoke, Virginia, after the war, and joined the Marine Corps Reserve in 1948 as a company commander. Less than two years later his unit was mobilized and sent to Korea, and he survived some of the war's most ferocious action, including fighting against the Chinese at the Chosin Reservoir. In this viewpoint, Hopkins describes how a call to active duty disrupts not only the lives of the reservist and his family, but also the lives of those in the community who depend on him. He also describes how he and some of his men came to join the Reserves and how their community saw them off to war.

The history of my own involvement in the Korean War began in 1940, when I enlisted in the U.S. Marine Platoon Leaders Class. I was a student at Washington and Lee University [in Lexington, Virginia] at the time. In April 1942, my senior year, I was called to active duty, and saw combat in the South Pacific before returning to the States in the summer of 1944. After the war I was honorably discharged as a captain in the inactive Marine Reserves.

I had been raised in Franklin County, Virginia. My father was a circuit judge, serving Franklin and Bedford counties. Until I was 12 years old, we lived in Rocky Mount, the county seat; then we moved to a farm six miles out of town. At an early age I decided to become a lawyer. So, after receiving my discharge from the Marine Corps in 1946, I entered the University of Virginia Law School at Charlottesville, Virginia. The law is a jealous mistress, and law school even more so. Although I read the daily newspapers, I gave little thought to what our country was doing, either right or wrong, in the field of foreign affairs.

During my stay in Charlottesville, I had met Ginny George, a recent graduate of Hollins College, near Roanoke. We became engaged. It had taken only a brief discussion for us to decide that Roanoke was the place where we wanted to live and practice law. So in January 1948, I hung out my shingle in Roanoke, sharing office space with two older lawyers. Office expenses were paid by searching titles for them. Although spending-money was hard to come by, Ginny and I decided to get married in June. Afterwards we rented a three-room apartment about two miles from my office. Neither of us owned an automobile, and on most occasions I walked to and from work to save the 20 cents bus fare.

Joining the Reserves

In late November 1948, Colonel Luther Brown, USMC, called at my office. He offered me the command of the 16th Marine

Reserve Engineer Company of Roanoke beginning January 1, 1949. At first I refused, saying I knew little about engineering, for I had been an infantry officer during World War II.

"Much of the training is on infantry and weapons subjects," he persisted. I continued to resist.

"You're paid a full day's pay for each two-hour drill, plus a quarterly supplement as company commander," he continued.

"Now you've placed the right bait on the hook," I replied. Soon I was shaking his hand in token of agreement.

I joined the Marine Corps Reserves primarily because I needed the extra money—but having done so I was determined to do the best I could with the company. Initially, after I took command, many members resigned because of the strict discipline demanded. I liked living in a democratic society, but in a military unit there was no place for democracy—fairness, yes; democracy, no. Those who stayed on had pride in the unit. By the fall of 1949 the company had again reached full strength, where it would remain. Our training classes and attendance at drill were taken quite seriously by the membership, even though no one believed that we would be called to active duty in the foreseeable future. We were totally unaware of how our nation's leaders were dealing with the problem of a little-known country called Korea.

Summer Camp

In May 1950 my company received orders to attend two weeks' summer camp at Little Creek, Virginia. Everyone was especially pleased that we would receive training in the Marine Corps' specialty, amphibious warfare. We left Roanoke early in the morning on June 24. When we arrived at Little Creek in midafternoon, the men were told that an inspection of quarters would be held at 0500 [that is, 5 o'clock the next morning]. Everyone who passed inspection could go on liberty immediately thereafter. By 0500 the bunks, lockers, rifles, and equipment were in tip-top shape.

Sunday, June 25, was a bright, sunny day at Little Creek. After breakfast most officers deserted the barracks to spend the day at Virginia Beach. I read the Sunday newspaper, wrote a long letter to Ginny, and then went swimming in the Officers' Club pool in the afternoon.

That evening I ate dinner alone at the Officers' Club. While sipping a drink, I watched the 6 o'clock news on the brand-new medium of television—still two years away for Roanoke. The announcer reported: "North Korean forces invaded Republic of Korea territory at several points this morning. It would appear from the nature of the attack and the manner in which it was launched that it constitutes an all-out offensive against the Republic of Korea. The United Nations Security Council met this morning at Lake Placid, New York, and is still in progress." What could this mean? No one knew; Korea was a long way off.

At Little Creek we spent two days on the rifle range, then concentrated on amphibious warfare. The noncoms [noncommissioned officers, or NCOs], mostly World War II vets, joked about the attitude of recruits going aboard ship. "I never thought they carried men across the ocean cooped up like this," many said. The consistent frontpage war headlines, however, caused our training to take on added significance.

A Rumor of War

The company officers celebrated the last night of summer encampment by dining at the Officers' Club. We were chatting when it was announced I had a long-distance phone call. Upon my return, I announced laughingly: "This you won't believe! That call came from Roanoke. A mother wanted to know if we were coming back tomorrow. She said there was a rumor back home that we were staying at Little Creek, maybe going to Korea!" All around the table broke out laughing at what we thought to be such a far-fetched idea.

Back in Roanoke, things settled back into routine. Yet there was uneasiness as the North Korean army drove deeply into South Korea, and American forces stationed in Japan joined the fray. On Monday, July 22, I came home early from work at my law office, took a shower, had a bite to eat, put on my uniform, and then drove hurriedly to the Marine Armory on Naval Reserve Avenue. When I reported for duty at 7 P.M., Captain James Einum, the inspector-instructor for the Roanoke Marines, met me at the door. "Bill, you've just received a telegram from the Commandant of the Marine Corps." He smiled as he handed it to me.

Called to Active Duty

Our company was ordered to active duty on August 10. We would travel by train to Camp Pendleton, Oceanside, California. At about this time Ginny would be going to the hospital; we expected our first child between August 5 and 10.

Having served in World War II, I knew what the telegram meant. Oceanside, California, was the jumping-off place to the Pacific. I read the message to Captain Ford Carmack, the company executive officer, Captain Leon Garber, the training officer, and First Lieutenant James Bear, platoon leader of the 1st Platoon, who were right behind me, then to the other officers as they arrived for duty that evening. All the officers had served with Marine units in the Pacific during World War II, and each showed deep concern.

I announced we would go ahead with drill and classes as usual. The telegram would not be read to the troops until everyone was ready to leave. After drill the company assembled in the auditorium. Jim Einum and the members of his staff were present. At 9:30, Ford Carmack reported that the men were waiting. Ford called them to attention when I appeared. I read the telegram:

"The 16th Marine Engineer Company is hereby called to active duty on the 10th day of August, 1950. Captain William

B. Hopkins, Commanding Officer, with all the men of the 16th Marine Engineer Company, will forthwith report to duty at the Marine Barracks, Camp Pendleton, Oceanside, California."

The words were no sooner out of my mouth than the men cheered, jumped up and down, beat their rifle butts into the floor, and threw their hats into the air. I thought to myself, What a damn bunch of fools! Great fools, but fools nonetheless.

Their reaction buoyed my spirits for the moment. After the company had been dismissed, everyone left for home; usually some of them stayed to chat or to gather at the beer joint down the street. I headed home to Ginny.

The war news continued bad from day to day. After the July 29 drill, I received another telegram from the Commandant, modifying the original order. Now the company would activate for duty on August 18, leave Roanoke on the 20th, and arrive at Camp Pendleton on the 24th. I welcomed this news, because Ginny would have been discharged from the hospital before we left for California.

Some Men Seek Deferments While Others Volunteer

There were numerous applications for discharges or deferments, but for each man discharged or deferred, a Marine veteran enlisted in his place. Physical examinations had to be given for each new enlistment. If a man had been honorably discharged as a platoon sergeant, and had a clean police record in the interim, he could re-enlist in the company at the same rank, provided that a vacancy existed. If there were none, he could accept a lower rank. The top NCO positions were quickly filled.

One World War II ex-platoon sergeant, from the adjoining County of Craig, when told that the highest rank available was corporal, decided to enlist anyhow. I told him I regretted that corporal was the best the company could do, and reminded him we might be getting orders for Korea soon after our arrival in California.

"That's fine with me if we go," he replied. "That's what I came here for. There ain't a damn thing over there as bad as living on a farm with a bitchy wife in Craig County!"

I took Ginny to the hospital on August 4. Our first child, a little girl, came on the morning of the 5th. We named her Catherine Dabney Hopkins, after my mother. Ginny's good old-fashioned doctor insisted she stay in the hospital for a full ten days. August 15, three days before our call to active duty, Ginny and Catherine Dabney left the hospital.

The last week was very busy with concerned parents, wives, or friends calling at my law office to discuss deferments. Some were justified, some not. In some instances we were able to do something about them, but in most we could not. Also, I had to close out my law office, after two and a half years of practice. I had obligations to my clients. In addition to being busy, I was worried about Ginny. Her parents were both dead, so my greatest problem was finding a place for her and the baby to stay. We decided on Rocky Mount, Virginia, where her sister, Nannie Saunders, lived. I lay awake every night, thinking about how I would say goodbye.

When the Sunday morning came, I arose early, had breakfast, and then went into the bathroom to wash up. Ginny followed close by. I kissed her goodbye, and closed my bag. Just as I did, she spotted one of her guest towels. "Don't you dare take that guest towel with you! You don't need it where you're going!" she exclaimed without shedding a tear. I gave her back the towel, got into my car, and drove to Roanoke.

The troops, except for one officer, Captain Bernard Schutt, assembled in front of the Marine Armory at 9 A.M. Schutt had received special orders which allowed him to drive his car to California. At roll call, two men were missing. Later we learned that one had been seriously injured in an automobile accident en route to the armory. The other had shot himself through the foot, and was admitted to a local hospital. The skies were overcast when we took our report. After roll call, the men loaded equipment on trucks to take [to] the train.

Marching Off to War

At 10 A.M., we began our two-mile march. One block from the Marine Armory, Naval Reserve Avenue runs into Jefferson Street, a main thoroughfare. The skies were still overcast. There were no bugles, drums, or music of any kind as we marched in silence down Jefferson Street. Gunnery Sergeant Paul Gibson, the type of Marine seen on recruit posters, and First Lieutenant Roy Kinsey, an excellent drill instructor, counted cadence when someone appeared out of step. A sprinkling of people gathered on either side. No one cheered, no one waved. Two-thirds of the way down Jefferson Street, at St. John's Episcopal Church, a crowd of Sunday churchgoers watched in silence as we passed.

The silence was broken three blocks from the Norfolk and Western Station. Kurt Fleming, a dapper, good-looking Roanoke College summer school student, stood in front of The Sportsman, a news and cigar store. An inactive Naval Reservist himself and a friend of some in the unit, Kurt shouted, "Have fun in Korea, fellows! Have fun! Don't worry about your women—I'll take care of them while you're gone!"

A few smiled, but gave no answer as we marched by at attention. When the column cleared The Sportsman, Kurt repeated, "Remember, don't worry about your women! I'll take care of them. Those I can't take care of myself, I have friends who can. Don't worry about your women while you're gone!"

At the station, a large crowd of relatives, friends, well-wishers, and others had gathered. My younger brother and father had come to see me off. . . . The overcast skies cleared while we exchanged pleasantries.

An old-time *Roanoke Times* reporter planted himself nearby. His story in the morning paper had read: "No flags will wave and no bands will play this morning as the Marine Reserves of Roanoke, its rank of rookies strengthened by veterans of Guadalcanal and Iwo Jima [famed World War II battle sites], leave for active duty." The reporter had his photographer take a picture of my father and me shaking hands. The caption in the next day's paper read, "Goodbye, and good luck, son!"

Many NCOs and officers, with their wives and children, formed a line to introduce family members, or just to shake hands before the train left. Corporal Paul Martin said proudly, "Cap'n, take a look at my baby boy; he's six weeks old tomorrow!"

"He looks like he's going to make a good football player like you, Paul!" I replied.

"I hope so," he smiled, as he passed with his pretty wife beside him.

"Good luck," she said in a soft voice.

By 11 o'clock it had turned into a bright day, with everyone looking happy, until the train actually began to move out of the station. Then many of the wives, mothers, and relatives broke into tears.

Remembering Good Things in a Bad War

James Brady

In some respects, the Korean War was the most difficult war the United States ever fought. Much of the fighting took place in the desolate mountainous regions of North Korea, where the winds from the Siberian steppes usher in subzero temperatures. After the Communist Chinese entered the war, the outnumbered Americans were driven back into South Korea despite mounting a stiff resistance, and this setback and subsequent permanent stalemate between North and South Korea fostered a sense of futility in many who saw little point to the loss of fifty-four thousand American lives. Furthermore, the concept of "limited war"—a war whose objective is less than the unconditional defeat of the enemy—failed to arouse a gung-ho spirit in many American servicemen. As the war dragged on, the primary goal of many became simple survival as much as helping a foreign ally repel a foreign enemy. Nevertheless, like most wars, the Korean War offered opportunities for soldiers to learn to enjoy unexpected pleasures.

In this selection, novelist and magazine columnist James Brady describes his experience in Korea as a twenty-three-year-old Marine lieutenant in command of a rifle platoon. His frank account of brutal conditions there, laced with rough language, is balanced by his appreciation of the rugged landscape and camaraderie among the troops. Brady's works about the Korean War include The Marine: A Novel of War from Guadalcanal to Korea, Warning of War: A Novel of the North China Marines, *and* The Scariest Place in the World: A Marine Returns to North Korea.

James Brady, *The Coldest War: A Memoir of Korea*. Hampshire, NY: Thomas Dunne, 1990. Copyright © 1990 by Superchic Media, Inc. All rights reserved. Reproduced by permission of the author and the author's agents, Scovil Chichak Galen Literary Agency, Inc.

When you weren't fighting, the war was pretty good. Mornings were the best time, the terror of night ended, the patrols and ambushes and duck blinds. Men slept late. When there was snow in the night, it lay smooth and untracked, no industrial smokestack or city's soot turning it dour and gray, no vehicles to churn it into slush. It hung, glistening, on the pine branches until the sun, warming as it rose, thawed it into tiny, shining icicles, glistening, melting, drop, drop, drop. Men crawled out of the bunkers into the morning calm, the industrious using entrenching tools to dig away the snow, tidying the trench. One imaginative fellow after each snow crafted a small snowman on the reverse slope a few yards from his bunker. Eventually there was a formation of them, a foot tall or so, some hunched gnomelike by earlier thaws, each with a cigar butt rakishly affixed in the center of a gargoyle's face. I passed them as I went down the slope for the morning dump. It was odd how you became hardened to almost anything, even that holed ammo box perched over its mingled scents of shit and creosote. You had lived through another night, you were healthy, your bowels were moving, the snowy hills stretched peacefully toward a horizon, the morning sun had begun to soften the hard chill of night. These were times of contemplation, ease, tranquility, with no decisions to be made or action to be taken. You just sat there and let it happen, totally passive, not having to work at it. Times like that were rare and wonderful, and even the stench became familiar and nearly welcomed.

Princeton [Brady's platoon sergeant], like most regulars, made a fetish of shaving daily. Water was always short. We melted snow in canteen cups over Coleman stoves and parceled it out from five-gallon jerricans. Maybe water is the heaviest thing marines ever have to carry. Do you know what five gallons of water weigh? Leftover coffee, just an ounce or two in the bottom of a cup, did for shaving. I was lucky, with a barely noticeable beard that an every-other-day shave kept clean. We never washed. There wasn't the water for that. I suppose we smelled pretty bad, but you stopped noticing. The air in the bunkers, lighted by candles and warmed by Coleman stoves, was so foul that you spit soot, and body odor didn't really register. You never changed clothes except for socks. I had two pairs of heavy wool socks and I tried to change every day. The socks you put on were filthy but after twenty-four hours they were dry, the sweat evaporated. Frozen feet were a continual fear; we all knew horror stories from the winter before; men who had lost toes or an entire foot, sometimes both feet. If you could somehow keep your feet dry, the cold wasn't as dangerous. You might, if the Koreans didn't get you, or a mine or an accidental discharge or a short round, survive the winter with limbs intact. How the socks smelled didn't matter, only that they were dry.

Leisurely Mornings

Mornings were coffee or cocoa, as hot as you could stand it, the ration cans of fruit, the syrup heavy and sugared. Unless there was serious shelling or heavy snow, after breakfast I walked the half mile along the ridgeline to the company command post to see Chafee [Brady's commanding officer] and Red Philips [Chafee's second in command]. The other platoon leaders came by, and Chafee gave us the orders and the situation and listened to complaints. Then we sat around gossiping, the way men do. By now it was maybe ten in the morning, and if the wind wasn't too bad we sat outside on the lip of the trench, smoking and talking, men easy with one another and relaxed. Night wouldn't fall for another six hours.

If there was mail from the gook train [the Korean supply system] I carried it back to the platoon stuffed inside my field jacket. Some men got a lot of mail; there were some who never got anything. You didn't ask. It was a man's own business; marines don't want people being sorry for them. That didn't mean I never wondered about it. By noon Princeton

Despite the brutal conditions of war, soldiers were able to enjoy a few simple pleasures.
Keystone/Hulton Archives/Getty Images

would have visited every bunker, inspecting weapons. The men could get dirty; the weapons had to be clean. If Chafee had ordered a patrol, Prince and the fortunate squad leader and I would lie in the snow with field glasses and a map and go over the route in daylight. It was funny, no matter what the weather, I was never cold by day. The nights were different; the nights were fierce.

When Princeton went off again on any of the thousand things a platoon sergeant did, busying himself, chivvying and prying, sometimes I just stayed out there somewhere sheltered from the wind and looked at the country, those serried rows of mountains, treed heavily lower down, sparser at top where granite pushed up through the earth, gray and cold, flinty looking and edged. If I had one, I smoked a cigar, chewing the stub into pulp, spitting juice onto the snow at my feet, onto my thermal boots. It didn't matter much; there were no inspections up here, none of the garrison chickenshit you lived with at [the marine bases at] Quantico [Virginia] or Pendleton [near San Diego, California] or even in reserve. These were good times too, afternoons looking at the mountains and the snow, and smoking and spitting with no one to complain, scratching yourself where you itched, your groin or your belly or wherever. In a country this lovely, unless someone was shooting at you or sending you out on patrol, if you could stay dry and warm, and you knew there was one more little can of sweet peaches or pears back in the bunker, the war wasn't so bad.

Then, by two thirty or two forty-five in the afternoon the sun would start to fall toward the ridgeline and the wind out of Siberia would pick up and I would begin to shiver, not just from cold but knowing that the good time was nearing its end, that darkness was coming, the dark and the night and the terrible cold and, unless we were lucky, the fighting. I hated to see the dusk come. In combat there are no beautiful sunsets; a falling sun is a warning of the night. The shadows lengthen and the temperature falls and the wind seeks you out. Men began to move around more now, restless, nervy, busying themselves with chores to take their minds off the night, breaking down weapons one more time for cleaning, rearranging the grenades and bringing in the sleeping bags left out for a day's airing, heating a supper of lima beans and ham before dark. Once the night comes there may not be time;

once the darkness falls the good times are past; the pleasant indolence, the contemplation of day is gone.

By four thirty there is no more sun and then only a swift dusk and then the real night, cold and frightening and, too often, deadly.

Desolate Countryside

I wondered what this country, these mountains and narrow valleys, was like in summer, without the snow and the killing wind. The pines and the spruce would be the same, of course, ever green and unchanged. But would other trees bloom and flowers grow on the ridges and the hillsides, would farmers work the river bottoms and the lower slopes, terracing the land into paddies, fertilizing the crop, as we were told they did, with human waste? And would the smell of shit float upward to the ridges from the rice fields below?

But there were no abandoned farmhouses here, no barns or silos, no huts or roads or telephone poles or fences and gates, no manmade structures of any kind. Despite snow cover, there should have been something; not even war flattened everything. There should have been ruins, a brick piled upon a brick, the remnant of a chimney, a lonely fence post. There were only the hills and the slim valleys and the evergreens and the snow, nothing else. This was simply not a country where anyone lived unless it was the wanderer passing through or a lone hunter carrying his tent and goods, his shotgun or his snares. But what would draw a hunter? We saw no game, not even a rabbit or a fox, nothing. Could the war have done that? Or had this always been a barren place?

Woodsmen might have come here. It was forest land, perhaps to be winnowed and harvested, the thunk of the woodsman's axe echoing against the hills. But there were no stumps, no patterned clearing that lumbering might have left. Amid the evergreens were other trees, and I wondered if they bloomed and grew leafy when the snow melted, sprouted lush green foliage and buds and flowers and maybe even fruit. Would we still be able to see that terrible 2,000-meter mountain that loomed so frighteningly just a few miles to our north? Or would the death that waited there be veiled by blossoms?

I hoped I would live until spring to see.

We were not to keep diaries. That was a rule. If you were killed or captured, a diary could provide military intelligence to the enemy. But I kept a few notes in the little spiral notebook in my breast pocket, writing very small to conserve pages, and in pencil. If you got wet, and we were always getting wet, ink ran. And I composed my letters home very carefully, describing as accurately as I could the land and the weather and the sense of place, on the cheap airmail flimsy they parceled out to us and which we could send without a stamp. There was supposed to be censorship, but I don't believe there ever was. Maybe in the rear echelons. Up here no one ever slit open a letter that I knew of. And so I wrote about Korea and the war and the men, self-censoring things that might frighten my family or friends, and sent off little essays and brief reports of war, knowing one day I might see those letters again and remember.

War Is Fun

It was not difficult to fill a letter without giving alarm. If you have never been to war you cannot realize that some of it— not all, of course—is such sheer, boyish fun. You lived outdoors, you were physically active, you shared the boisterous camaraderie of other young men, you shed fat and put on sinew and muscle. Except for those nagging, minor hurts, you were clear-eyed and generally healthy, and your body responded, instantly and instinctively, whenever called upon. You slept like the dead; not even the dull menu of the ration box killed appetite. You saw the dawn and the night stars and came to calculate time and date by the phases of the moon, and on those rare days of thaw, you heard the gurgle of running water under the snow, heading toward the valleys and the sea. You smelled the pines and listened to the wind and could sense when snow was coming and knew to the instant when the sun would rise, when the sun would set.

A city boy, I was falling in love with country those first months in the hills.

If only I would get home to tell about it.

Life as an American Prisoner of War in Korea

Donald M. Elliott

The entry of the Communist Chinese into the Korean War in October 1950 caught many American units off guard. At this point, four months after North Korea's invasion of South Korea, U.S. forces had pushed the North Koreans back and advanced almost to the border between North Korea and China. When they were engaged by the Chinese, the Americans were not only thinly stretched across the North but also greatly outnumbered. Some seventy-two hundred Americans were captured by the Chinese and held in prisoner-of-war (POW) camps until the end of the war. The American POWs were subjected to extremely harsh conditions; 39 percent died in captivity, mostly from starvation. By comparison, only 4 percent of American POWs died in German camps during World War II, and the death rate at the hands of the Japanese in WWII, whose treatment of POWs was internationally condemned as barbarous, was 34 percent.

Donald M. Elliott served in Korea as a private first class in the U.S. Army's Second Division. His duty assignment was switchboard operator in the communications section of a headquarters company. On the night of May 18, 1951, his two-thousand-man unit was overrun by an estimated eighty thousand Chinese and Elliott and about eight hundred other American soldiers were captured. He spent the next twenty-seven months in a succession of POW camps. In this viewpoint, Elliott describes the long marches, freezing temperatures, poor food, inadequate shelter, and indifferent medical treatment that contributed to the high death rate of American POWs in the Korean War.

Harry Spiller, ed., *American POWs in Korea: Sixteen Personal Accounts*. Jefferson, NC: McFarland, 1998.

At about 2:00 A.M. when I was relieved from the switchboard, I made a trip out of the switchboard area. The switchboard was a trench and dugout area into the side of a rice paddy with a shelter-half hanging over the entrance. I went to the latrine. As I returned to the dugout I realized the Chinese troops were in our area. I started running. I tripped over something on the ground and fell flat on my face. That no doubt was the most fortunate fall I ever had because as I started to get up a Chinese fired about ten rounds at me. I ended up with a face full of dirt but not hit. After lying a short while and looking around, I continued on crawling the 20 yards or so back to the dugout. The next adventure was only about four hours later. The switchboard crew was joined during the night by two of our battalion-forward communications detachment men who had been caught in a firefight and had been sent back to the rear for a good night's sleep. We also had some South Korean supply people in the bunker. They had been hired by the army to carry supplies from regiment headquarters to points forward. When sunrise came I became aware of a Korean supply carrier sitting right next to me. I didn't know if he was Korean or Chinese so for probably 30 minutes my bayonet was a few inches from his ribs. Had he turned out to be Chinese, I was prepared to shove the bayonet into him.

Captured

After daylight, it became obvious that we were surrounded. For a couple of hours the Chinese were running through the area. One of them had a trumpet and played taps on it over and over for an hour. I was on the telephone with the battalion executive major when he bought the farm [died] from a machine gun. At 6:10 A.M. a burst of burp gun was fired through the shelter-half that covered the entrance to our dugout-switchboard area. I guess I will always remember the circle pattern of the burp gun blast. There were nine rounds fired, there were nine people in the dugout, and the Korean beside me got all nine rounds. He didn't even moan.

Immediately the two men from battalion forward started calling out "surrender" and "prisoner." They then started filing out of the dugouts with their hands in the air. Because I was the person on duty I was sitting the farthest from the entrance and was the last to leave. Immediately after we filed out of the dugout a North Korean [N.K.] soldier wanted to shoot all eight of us. The Chinese troops actually jerked his weapon away and booted the N.K. in the behind and sent him away from us.

I guess I was lucky as compared to some. Jim O'Boyle from a different outfit was captured on May 15 in a firefight. He was held by the Chinese for three days before being brought south during their big push. The Chinese told him to keep going when they crossed our original defense line. He checked in at headquarters rear. Someone handed him a rifle and sent him forward. He spent part of the night with us before being captured along with the rest of us. It was the second time he had been captured in three days. Jim died of diphtheria in February 1952 while in Camp Three.

The March: May 18, 1951–October 8, 1951. They captured about 800 troops from all companies of the 2nd Division. Because of the large number of POWs we were constantly moving from place to place trying to find enough food. We spent the first night in an abandoned Korean hut while we waited for more and more POWs to be assembled. The second night we spent in a cave with very little air. We went in after dark, and there wasn't enough air to burn a match. The rumor circulated that the entrance to the cave was going to be closed off and we were all going to die. But it was just a rumor.

About noon the next day the Chinese started taking us out of the caves. The UN Air Force was conducting an air strike in the region. In groups of four and five we had to crawl out of the cave and then run about 50 yards to a forest area for protection from the bombs. We walked and carried the wounded for days. There was little food, and some of the men were wounded badly. As we marched they just wasted away, and within the first eight days men started dying—one or two a day. We made our way north, mostly walking at night and resting anyplace we could find during the day. It was May 30 and we were walking in the early evening. It started raining real hard. I was a long way from the front line and I didn't see what happened, but the story that circulated went like this. The lead guard stopped to ask directions of either a Korean or another Chinese soldier and was told we should stay to the right at a Y in the path. We spent all night slipping and falling and trying to climb a very high mountain in the rain. The next morning when it quit raining and we couldn't find our destination we were told we took the wrong trail the night before. At that point the guards were either very tired themselves or showed some compassion for the conditions because we rested for a full 24 hours before we retraced our steps and crossed the mountains going the other way to return to the spot where we took the wrong turn.

One very helpful incident occurred near the end of the return trip: an officer of the Chinese army passed out and was lying beside the trail as we all walked past. That was a real morale booster. The GIs [American soldiers] started singing marching songs and managed to stay happy for a few hours. The guards were happy that we were happy but didn't have a clue for the reason.

We walked for about three or four weeks and those of us who were left finally made it to the first stop—the Bean Camp.

The Bean Camp. Our first extended stop was at the Bean Camp. The camp got the name because of the diet—almost exclusively they fed us soybeans. We thought our diet had improved when we got to the camp because of the soybean diet.

Up until that time we had been eating "bug dust," a millet or sorghum grain with kidney beans in the sorghum. Bug dust is a very fine powder made up of the brown outer shell of rice when it is polished to make it like the rice we are familiar with. Later we found out that soy beans must be boiled for several hours to break down the hard outer shell. The Chinese either didn't know or didn't care or didn't have the time properly to cook the soy beans. The improperly cooked soybeans will pass through the digestive system very rapidly and in the process tear up everything on the way. Within two days every POW had diarrhea or dysentery. When my dysentery started, I quit eating the beans and just used the liquid they were cooked in. We stayed at the Bean Camp for three or four weeks before we started marching again. By the time we left I had gotten rid of my dysentery, but many of the GIs hadn't. When we started to march again they were too weak and they'd started dying.

The Mining Camp. We arrived at the Mining Camp on July 3, 1951. With the exception of about one death per day and the bastard doctor who sold the little bit of medicine he was given to care for us, things were much better at this camp. We had a roof over our heads and enough room to lie down to sleep. The food improved some, with occasional rice and canned meat.

At the Bean Camp the Chinese had started a little bit of indoctrination, but when we got to the Mining Camp indoctrination was held every day. It was the good of all the people with Communism, and capitalism was for the few rich. No one was taking it seriously. Then, after a couple of months, on September 20, 1951, the Chinese moved us again.

Camp One: October 1951–August 1953. The Chinese army moved the civilians out of their homes, and we moved in. The town was Chon Chin, a good-sized town. We were issued student uniforms and had an opportunity to wash clothes and get rid of the lice we had been living with since about June of '51. The lice eggs needed body heat to hatch, so as soon as we were able to wash clothes and get them off our bodies the new lice quit hatching and we were able to live without lice.

There were about 30 huts, with two to three rooms each and ten GIs per room. The rooms were about 10 by 15 feet. We ate, slept, spent all our time this way. The only change was "brainwashing" sessions and a few work details. Most of those were gathering firewood for heating and cooking. We also had about 100 British troops across the road. No fences.

The guards experienced night blindness starting about November and lasting until late April when we started eating fresh vegetables again. Many of the POWs also had night blindness because of poor diet with little or zero vegetables.

Regardless of how bad things are for a person you can always find someone who has it worse. I was near the Chinese kitchen and saw a blind Korean woman trying to find food for her self and a naked baby that was about nine months old. She was sitting in the garbage pile sifting through the garbage with her hands. Because of her blindness every little piece she picked up had to go to her nose and mouth for sampling. After the test, if she thought it was of some value it went into a very small gourd bowl. If she didn't think it was edible, it went back into the pile. It was a heart-breaking sight, but one that helped me because I actually realized that even though I was a prisoner of war I was lucky compared with her.

In 1952 the peace talks were going well and things in the camp began to get better. The medical care improved enough that if someone got sick and went to sick call and ended up in the hospital we didn't tell them goodbye. Prior to this the sick and wounded simply died if the other GIs couldn't take care of them. A few died after 1952 but not like before. As best that we could figure, of the approximately 800 captured between May 18, 1950, and May 20, 1951, 54 percent died as a result of wounds or dysentery while we were marching from place to place trying to find enough food.

I had two incidents that happened to me with the doctors. The first incident happened in February 1952 when I came down with a deep chest cold. Always, when I had a chest cold when I was younger, asthma was not far behind. The asthma came this time, but by now we had sick call in the camp. Because I had had a life-long problem with asthma I had a good idea how it should be controlled. I went to sick call and explained to the doctor what my treatment should be. The doctor had heard of asthma but had never treated anyone. I explained that first we must treat the cold, then, to relieve the symptoms of the asthma, adrenaline-in-oil would relieve the wheezing. To my surprise he provided the sulfa drug for the cold and further, he advised that he didn't have the adrenaline but he would get it. We talked for 30–45 minutes. I felt like he had a sincere interest in my problem and was very much wanting to learn from me about asthma. The sulfa did its job in about three days, and then for the next two days he called me to sick call to administer the adrenaline. The combination worked, and I was careful not to catch a cold again.

Diarrhea and Frozen Toes

The second incident dealt with the general condition of my body. We were eating only two meals a day at the time, and I had been having diarrhea for about six months. The diet was vastly different from what GIs were accustomed to eating, and nearly everyone had some problems with their digestive systems, not to mention all the other problems too numerous to describe. During one very cold spell, 40–50 degrees below zero, my diarrhea got much worse. During the 24-hour period, I made 32 trips to the outhouse. It was outside and about 20 feet from our hut. The diarrhea improved, but these trips in the cold plus the lack of heat in the hut took their toll on us. About two or three weeks later, they let me have some water and I tried to clean up a little. I took off my shoes and socks and discovered three frozen toes. They were black on the ends. I went to sick call thinking I was going to lose my toes. Instead, the doctor started scraping the ends of my toes. I started sick call visits each day, and a nurse would put on a black tarlike substance on my toes to draw out the infection. Every other visit they would put sulfur powder on my toes to heal them. It worked. By the time the infection was gone my toes were healed. Very primitive, but it worked. A side benefit of all this was that the Chinese cooks got a big cast-iron pot, put it in our kitchen, and we had heat. They and our cooks used the hot water to cook.

If you were quiet enough you could walk by the guards because of the poor eyesight, so a few GIs were shot or shot at during the November–April time periods. The turnips helped everyone's night blindness, and after that the guards weren't so jumpy.

At this camp the indoctrination increased to twice a day, except during the cold weather. The most concentrated effort took place in late summer through fall of 1952. They tried very hard to convince us that the U.N. troops were using germ warfare. They set up a display of bugs, bomb fragments, and pictures to convince us. We had about five or six weeks of this constant preaching about germ warfare, then we saw the display, and finally we took a written test to see how much we had learned. We heard a rumor that in Camp Five one of the prisoners swallowed one of the bugs and the Chinese starved him for two weeks to be sure he got sick, but they finally gave up. He was really hungry, but he didn't get sick.

After we took the test about germ warfare, the Chinese were unhappy with our lack of learning and stopped most of the brainwashing. One of the interpreters called me to head-quarters to ask why I didn't believe that germ warfare had been used. I told him if our military were using germ warfare we would all be dead. He told me I had a bad attitude and sent me back to my hut.

In the spring of 1952 we asked for vegetables, and the Chinese got a truckload of turnips. We had 101 meals of boiled turnips (two meals a day for 50 days).

Don Gets in Trouble Because of His First Name

By 1953, things continued to improve. The living conditions, diet, and the opportunity to play a little baseball were part of it. One of the things that always amazed me was how much difficulty two different cultures can have communicating. I can remember an incident that is funny now, but it wasn't at the time. The Chinese were constantly accusing us of crimes against the common people's republic. As a consequence of this, various GIs were suddenly arrested, and as a result of these arrests they usually were moved away from our camp. We seldom ever saw the arrested person again. One evening in the early spring of '53 at an evening formation the camp commander, whom we rarely saw, announced the arrest of Donald . . . Bittner, for crimes undisclosed. I and all the others with the first name of Donald had a uh-oh feeling as the interpreter paused between the first and last name for at least 15 seconds. Bittner was arrested and removed from the formation, never to be seen in our camp again. After the formation broke up, we all returned to our squad rooms. Joe Bramantti, a big mouth, called to me from two rooms away: "Well, they almost got you this time, didn't they?" I didn't say much because just at about that time we became aware that one of the interpreters was standing outside the door listening to our babble. At 3:00 A.M. a guard came after me. I will always believe it was because of Joe's wisecrack, but what we will never know is why the guard was there in the first place. For the next three days I learned a lot about what was going on around the camp. First, the Chinese believed that I and my followers had burned down the rec-room they had just built for us. Someone threw a rock through the window of the Chinese headquarters telling the Chinese that they had better shape up or be shipped out. Several other incidents were supposed to have happened, according to the Chinese, and I was supposed to be the ringleader of it all. Several others had been arrested and were suspected as ringleaders also. I was questioned and accused by a Chinese officer for several hours. The officer drank tea and smoked constantly as he questioned me, and then suddenly he left the room with papers scattered all over his desk. Very strangely, of all the papers on the desk there was only one in English. I asked myself why a Chinese interpreter would leave that paper if he didn't want me to read it. Well, I read it. It was a list of bad guys in my group. All these guys were the people who had been arrested and removed from camp in the last year or so, including Don Bittner. I will never know if my confession was better than the rest, but I was not arrested and removed from the camp like the rest of the so-called bad guys had been. When the Chinese interpreter returned, he told me that I should stand at attention and consider the error of my ways and my crimes against the common people's republic. I considered it at attention for 34 hours straight. At the end of that time I was given a paper and pen and told to write my confession. The first attempt took three or four hours and involved about four pages. I did not implicate anyone except the others on the list and only wrote in generalities about the crimes against the people. After my first attempt I was offered a cigarette and tea. I took the tea, but refused the cigarette and it unnerved the interpreter. I guess he didn't realize that all GIs didn't smoke. After another hour to two and some food, I was told that my confession was not sincere enough or long enough so I should do it again. This time I used every big word I could think of, spread the words out, increased the space between the lines and wrote the same thing. It increased the length to seven pages. After a short pause I was told to return to my hut, and I was never bothered again. . . .

Operation Big Switch: Repatriation, August 1953

We were trucked to the Yalu River and the northeast corner of North Korea to a train terminal, put on cattle cars, and rode the only restored train track from the extreme northeast corner of North Korea to Panmunjom. At the peace talks it was agreed that after a certain stage in the talks, the UN troops would not bomb this railroad right-of-way so that the Communists could rebuild it for aiding the repatriation of the prisoners.

After arriving at the camp at Panmunjom, we ate pretty good. Our diet had improved vastly in the last month, since the peace talks made it look like things were going to be settled. We spent one night at their camp, and after breakfast the next morning we were loaded on trucks and moved to the area set up at Panmunjom for the exchange of prisoners. One of the articles of the peace agreements included a no-man's-zone of probably 500 yards that each prisoner had to walk across to prove his intent that he wanted to be repatriated. The odds were a little lopsided. Twenty-one GIs refused repatriation, and 50,000–70,000 Chinese and North Koreans refused.

After crossing the line, we were greeted by a U.S. Army general who saluted and shook our hands. Close behind the general was an American flag. I and many others broke into tears when we saw the American flag waving in the breeze. We then went into a tent and were given time to spend with a chaplain.

The next stop was a hot shower and new clothes. Then we went to bed to relax. Nurses brought us a list of foods we could have. I remember the roast beef, mashed potatoes, gravy, corn, bread and butter, milk, and apple pie à la mode. It was wonderful.

The next day my jaw started swelling. I had not used the right side of my mouth for over a year because of bad teeth. I was given penicillin for one week before the dentist pulled two badly infected teeth.

The next day we were loaded on helicopters ten at a time and were airlifted to the port of Inchon. After the 30 minute ride, we were loaded on small boats and were taken out to a troopship anchored in the harbor.

The next day we sailed for home. There were probably 200 repatriated prisoners on the ship and about 2,000–3,000 regular returning troops. We were kept on a separate deck of the ship. We were not allowed to mix with the other troops. We even had our own mess hall. We had a special diet, along with a number of pills that we had to take. The other troops were always watching us, and we had fun acting strange in front of them.

During the two-week boat ride, we kept busy being interviewed by doctors about our treatment. Because there had been a few prisoners who had refused repatriation we were all suspect of no-telling-what. Every one of us had an individual sit-down with the psychiatrist. I'm not sure, but I think I am the only one out of the 200 who didn't have to go back for three or four more sessions. I didn't have anything to hide, and I told the psychiatrist everything I knew and what I thought about it. Many of the GIs were coy and didn't open up, which the doc saw through right away. Before it was over, he told us that most would not have problems adjusting to civilian life. We had a few group sessions before it ended.

We pulled into San Francisco harbor, under the Golden Gate Bridge, and docked at the Presidio area. It was a wonderful sight and a wonderful day. My mom and dad and other family members were waiting on the dock. We had a great time, and after a day of processing we caught a plane home.

Racial Prejudice Against African American Soldiers in the Korean War

William T. Bowers, William M. Hammond, and George L. MacGarrigle

The U.S. Army's Twenty-fourth Infantry Regiment was histori-cally an all-black unit. Formed in 1869, the unit served with distinction against Indians in the American West, the Spanish in Cuba, insurrectionists in the Philippines, Pancho Villa's forces in Mexico, and the Japanese in the South Pacific during World War II. Nevertheless, the unit was constantly under threat of disband-ment because of the prevailing racist attitude that black troops were poor troops. The unit was dispatched to Korea after its members received some rudimentary training in Japan, but for the most part its (white) commanding officers were unenthusias-tic about their assignments. Nor surprisingly, the Twenty-fourth performed poorly in combat in Korea, so poorly that Major Gen-eral William B. Kean, commander of the Twenty-fifth Infantry Division (to which the Twenty-fourth was attached), officially recommended that the Twenty-fourth be disbanded because it was "untrustworthy and incapable of carrying out missions ex-pected of an infantry regiment." On October 1, 1951, the Twenty-fourth was disbanded and its personnel reassigned to other units.

In 1992 military historians William T. Bowers, William M. Hammond, and George L. MacGarrigle were asked by the U.S. Army's Center of Military History to determine, if possible, whether Kean's charges against the Twenty-fourth were justified. They published their findings in Black Soldier, White Army: The 24th Infantry Regiment in Korea, *in which they conclude that the poor leadership and racism of the unit's white officers were major causes of the unit's failure in combat. In the follow-*

William T. Bowers, William M. Hammond, and George L. MacGarrigle, *Black Soldier, White Army: The 24th Infantry Regiment in Korea*. Washington, DC: Center of Military History, U.S. Army, 1996.

ing viewpoint, Bowers, Hammond, and MacGarrigle describe the valor of several men of the Twenty-fourth and blame the vulnerability of the unit on the regiment's colonel and several other white officers.

Combat, 5 August 1950

It rained heavily the next day, 5 August. All battalions [of the 24th] began to patrol their areas while holding reaction forces in reserve to counter any enemy threat that developed. Units of the 1st Battalion apprehended six South Korean deserters but made no contact with the enemy. The 2d Battalion also sent out patrols that failed to result in action, but it suffered one casualty in a strafing attack by an unidentified aircraft during the early morning hours. The 3d Battalion launched its patrols toward Sobuk-san, a large hill five miles to the south of Haman, where one took a prisoner. The man revealed that approximately 200 enemy soldiers were in the vicinity. At 1500 with rain continuing, the 3d Battalion's commander, Colonel [Samuel] Pierce, moved out to engage the force. He was accompanied by his intelligence and operations officers, an artillery liaison party headed by Capt. Alfred F. Thompson, Company L reinforced with a portion of Company I and elements from Company M, and the battalion's attached company of South Koreans. In all, he had the better part of a battalion at his disposal.

The force rode part of the way toward Sobuk-san on vehicles loaned by the 159th Field Artillery Battalion. During the trip out, the battalion operations officer, Capt. John B. Zanin, broke off with a patrol of five men to reconnoiter the area. Discovering after dark that he was separated from Pierce's main force by an enemy unit of unknown size, Zanin took evasive action until dawn and then led his men back to friendly lines on his own.

Moving forward, elements of the rest of the battalion task force encountered and dispersed a small enemy party. At dusk

Pierce dispatched a platoon from Company L to determine whether a nearby village contained more North Korean troops. The platoon leader, white 1st Lt. Sandro A. Barone, a newly arrived combat veteran of World War II, noted that his troops "were noisy and seemed untrained in night patrolling." A short while later, determining that no enemy were in the village, the platoon returned to Pierce's position.

Meanwhile, the rest of the battalion had halted on the approaches to a small plateau south of the village. The battalion staff, company command elements, and many of the officers gathered in a hollow to await the return of the patrols and to discuss what to do next. Inertia grew. No one laid out defensive positions, and Pierce himself went to sleep. "They were all just sort of sitting around," black 1st Lt. Oliver Dillard recalled. "No one seemed in command, and the troops, of course, had been told to stop, and when troops are told to stop, as they do in the Army today, they just stop where they are and go to sleep, resting on their packs."

Company L Breaks and Runs

After dark, just as Barone's platoon was rejoining the battalion, a small group of North Koreans estimated to number fewer than thirty men pushed quietly to within small-arms range of the unit and opened fire with automatic weapons. Whether the South Koreans or the men of Company L broke first is unclear. What is known is that after a brief fight both groups fled down the hill, overturning two jeeps in the process and abandoning a radio, a number of M1 rifles and carbines, and most of their heavy weapons. Pierce was shot in both legs. Company L's recently arrived commander, black Capt. Rothwell W. Burke, was killed along with two enlisted men. Eleven American soldiers were wounded and two were listed as missing and [were] never recovered. Losses among the South Koreans are unknown.

African American soldiers, like these in the U.S. Army's 24th Infantry Regiment, experienced racism at the hands of their white superiors. Breeding/Time Life Pictures/Getty Images

White officers would later use the incident as one indication that the men of the 24th Infantry had lost their nerve. In fact, if Company L and its attached units were routed, the officers were as much to blame as those who had run. Pierce had allowed his troops to wait for several hours in the dark without insisting that they establish defensive positions or guard against surprise attack. It was a surefire formula for disaster, especially when troops who were already tired and skittish faced an enemy who had turned the tactics of the unexpected into a fine art.

Two Men Perform Bravely

Whatever the condition of the unit as a whole, some of its men were clearly willing to stand their ground. Pfc. William Thompson of Company M, for one, covered the retreating force with his machine gun. Hit repeatedly by enemy grenade fragments and small-arms fire, he refused the entreaties of comrades to withdraw and continued to lay down covering fire until his company was clear of the area and he was mortally wounded. But for him, casualties that day might have been far worse. In the same way, rifleman George Bussey and others saw to it that the wounded Pierce reached safety. Thompson received a posthumous Medal of Honor for his valor and two other men received Silver Stars, but the action was, in many respects, a dismal and embarrassing defeat.

Combat, 6 August 1950

By 0230 on 6 August the men of Pierce's force were beginning to congregate at Haman, five miles to the rear. They would continue to straggle in throughout the morning. At 0915 Company I, reinforced with one platoon from the 77th Engineer Combat Company, attempted to return to the area of the attack to collect lost weapons and to search for the missing. Encountering the enemy in strength before reaching that goal, the force was pinned down by intense small-arms and mortar fire. In the ensuing engagement, Company I became separated from the engineers. Many of its men headed south to Chindong-ni where they joined up with other American units.

Trailing Company I, the engineer platoon, under black 2d Lt. Chester Lenon, was also pinned down. Lenon sought to eliminate the enemy's machine guns with grenades but fell wounded in the attempt. Staying behind to cover his platoon's withdrawal, he hid for five days along with six wounded enlisted men. A seventh, Pfc. Edward Sanders, sometimes crawling, sometimes walking, eluded enemy patrols to make his way eight miles to the rear to seek help. Bitten by a poisonous snake during the journey and terribly swollen as a result, the man was found by an American patrol on 11 August, five days after he and his comrades had been written off as dead. When informed, the commander of the unit, 1st Lt. Charles Bussey, set out immediately with two platoons to rescue the lost men. When he arrived, he found that two had died. Burying them temporarily on the spot, he delivered the others to the regimental clearing station.

The 24th Gets a New Commander

On 5 August, while Company L was suffering its ordeal, General [William B.] Kean had relieved Colonel [Horton V.] White as commander of the 24th Infantry and had appointed Col. Arthur S. Champeny to take his place. Present at the regimental command post when White had received the word, the operations officer of the 159th Field Artillery Battalion, Maj. Cloyd V. Taylor, remarked that Kean's move clearly had come as no surprise to White and that the officer seemed glad to hear the news. His exertions had been too much for him, Taylor said. He had lost a great deal of weight and seemed almost gaunt.

At fifty-seven years of age, Champeny was four years older than Kean himself, but he was an experienced combat commander. He had won a Distinguished Service Cross and the French Croix de Guerre during World War I and had commanded the 351st Infantry regiment of the 88th Infantry Division for thirty-two months during World War II. While leading the unit in Italy during the Cassino campaign of 1944, he had received a second Distinguished Service Cross. Following the end of the war, he had served as deputy commander of the U.S. Military Government in Korea, a position that had required him to wear the star of a brigadier general even though he had not at that time been promoted to the rank. When the Korean War broke out, he was serving at the Boston Army Base. Identified as a proven regimental commander because of his experience in the two world wars, he was immediately assigned to Korea. A man of "amazing energy and courage," according to the 25th Division artillery commander, Brig. Gen. George B. Barth, he was also "peppery and brutally frank."

Champeny Insults the Troops

Champeny's combat experience notwithstanding, he got off to a bad start with the 24th. At noon on the day after taking command, becoming aware of the misfortune that had befallen Pierce's unit near Sobuk-san, he called together those portions of the 3d Battalion that were present at Haman and delivered an angry dressing down. Correspondent James L. Hicks of the *Baltimore Afro-American* was nearby and later told investigators what he had heard. "He got up and told them . . . that he had been in the 88th [Division] in Italy, and at that time he had an element of the [all-black] 92d [Infantry] Division attached to him, and he said that this was the outfit that had a reputation for running, and they ran all over Italy, and he said that his observations had proved that colored people did not make good combat soldiers, and that his job down there was to change the frightened 24th into the fighting 24th." Hicks continued that a number of the men present had been in the 92d and had not run and that they had left the meeting insulted and angry. "I went to Champeny," Hicks said, "and asked him why he made the statement such as he did, and he said 'I said it . . . Isn't it the truth?' Those were his very words. It almost knocked me out. . . . He said that he did not intend to insult my race. He was only trying to make those men so mad that they would really get mad enough to fight."

The Troops Respond

Champeny's hard-boiled approach, if that is what it was, appears to have split the men of the regiment into two groups. On one hand, many knowledgeable blacks and even some whites resented the colonel's methods. Years later, the white intelligence officer of the 1st Battalion, Capt. Gustav Gillert, observed that Champeny's remarks demonstrated the colonel's "misunderstanding of the combat situation and the poor tactical condition of the regiment." They "appalled me and others," he continued, "who had put our anatomies on [the] line over the previous two months and were working hard at motivation and personal leadership." Sgt. Daemon Stewart of the intelligence and reconnaissance platoon recalled that Champeny was one of the worst officers he encountered during his military career. Rifleman Charlie Lee Jones, who was present for Champeny's speech, observed that many of the men believed the colonel was bluffing and from then on declined to place any trust in him. "If you don't trust officers," he added, "you won't fight for them." On the other hand, the regiment's awards and decorations officer, black 2d Lt. Clinton Moorman, recalled that Champeny was fairly well respected; Zanin considered him a topnotch commander; and Hicks himself remarked that he considered the officer the victim of an ill-advised impulse. "Col. Champeny is a brave and a hard working man," he said. "I had to get out there at 5:30 A.M. to catch him, and he would stay out until 9:00 o'clock [P.M.], but it takes time to take these unfortunate things down."

The 1st Battalion operations officer at the time, black Capt. Richard W. Williams, Jr., was hardly as generous. Implying in sworn testimony before an Eighth Army inspector general that the colonel was a bigot, he gave an example of what he meant. "One time, when I was commanding 'Charlie' Company, I had a position organized and had white and colored NCO's [noncommissioned officers] and Negro and ROK [South Korean] troops. Col. Champeny told me to build a wire enclosure around the hill with a six-foot opening, so the colored troops wouldn't run, and if they did run, they would hurt themselves. He also stated in front of many of those people that he would not have a Negro NCO in charge of ROK troops and white troops." Champeny later confirmed in an interview that on 6 September he had indeed ordered double-apron wire fences constructed around the 1st Battalion to "impress upon the men ... that if they would remain in their fox holes, they would not get hurt."

Racial Insults

Whatever Champeny's intentions, his approach did nothing to restrain those among the unit's white officers who were inclined to racial prejudice. According to Williams, several instances occurred during the weeks that followed, while intense combat raged, in which those individuals ridiculed the men of the regiment instead of encouraging them. "This caused the troops to lose confidence in themselves," Williams said. "Then they lost all hope."

LIVING THROUGH
THE COLD WAR

CHAPTER 3

The Korean Experience

Life as a North Korean Refugee

Young Sik Kim

The Korean War displaced countless numbers of Koreans on both sides of the 38th parallel, the boundary between North and South Korea. Many of these displaced people found their way to U.S.-sponsored refugee camps in South Korea, where conditions were sometimes only slightly better than those they had fled. Many refugees later found work with the South Korean or U.S. governments and eventually made their way to the United States, where they settled permanently.

Young Sik Kim was one such refugee, born in 1935 in Kapsan, a remote village in northern Korea. Following the rise of Kim Il Sung as dictator of North Korea, Kim joined the Student Volunteers Army (Hamhung Unit), an anti-Communist paramilitary group composed mostly of high school students from the North Korean city of Hamhung. During the war his group went to South Korea to fight alongside the South Korean army, but there his unit was disarmed and disbanded and Kim became a civilian refugee. After the war he landed a job as an interpreter with the U.S. Counter Intelligence Corps. In 1955 he came to the United States and eventually settled in Columbus, Ohio. In this viewpoint Kim describes the conditions in the various refugee camps in which he lived during the conflict.

Dec. 31, 1950—We arrive at the island of Koje. The first stop is Jisepo. Jisepo was a naval base during the Yi dynasty [of Korea], but it is now a fishing village. It is blessed with a natural harbor with a large lagoon. Its climate is mild and the seashores team with edible seaweed and shellfish—an ideal location for war refugees. Its population is probably less than 2,000. Over one hundred US army tents are erected for

Young Sik Kim, "Eyewitness: A North Korean Remembers," www.kimsoft.com.

N Korean refugees on the beach. The refugees from Hungnam are dropped off and we head for Jangsepo, the administrative center of Kojedo.

The Student Volunteers Army Reaches South Korea

Jangsepo—We finally reach our destination. Jansepo has a larger population than Jisepo and has some modern buildings. A group of S Korean police come aboard. We are shocked to notice that they are wearing the Japanese police uniforms—black cap and black cloth. They have even retained the Japanese name—Gei-sha-tzu! I guess the N Koreans were not lying about the S Korean police being made of Jap collaborators. This is not a good start—maybe we have made a big mistake switching side?

The policemen don't want a bunch of armed N Koreans (meaning us, the Student Volunteers Army) landing here. Why pick Jangsepo? No one knows for sure who has the authority to decide. Who will pay for our lodging and food? Refugees are taken care of by the UN [United Nations]. S Korean soldiers are taken care of by the Army. Who are responsible for us? We are neither refugees nor soldiers.

Some guys think that the Education Minister is our boss (after all we are the 'Student' Volunteers Army), but others think that the Defense Minister is our boss (we are the Student Volunteers 'Army'). Our commander is called into the discussion and starts negotiating. The Navy captain has his orders to move on to another assignment and wants to unload us right away. The village chief wants a written order from the central government.

After a long heated meeting, the policemen agree to let us land and provide a temporary lodging to us. They want custody of all of our weapons. They also want a written order from a S Korean authority clarifying what we are doing here as soon as possible. Our commander gives in to the police. He agrees to donate all the rice and other supplies we have brought from Hamhung. The navy captain agrees to take the commander to Pusan—the war time seat of [South Korean president] Syngman Rhee's government. The commander says he knows some important people and will be back with funds and the official papers in a few days.

We are led to a small abandoned warehouse—our new quarters. Our bedding is a sleeping bag on a hardwood floor. We are divided into groups of 4 and assigned to a 'patriotic' family. The poor locals are 'volunteered' to feed a group until our commander comes back with funds. We are not exactly welcome guests to the locals. The locals are dirt poor themselves, eking out a living doing who knows what. Our meals consist of potato plants (no potatoes!), seaweed, boiled barley and some other foul smelling stuff.

Jan. 12—Our Student Volunteers Army (SVA) detachment is made of an odd mix of people from N Korea. Everyone of us has a different reason why he has fled to south. There are deserters from the N Korean Army. They escaped from the Nakdong front and went into hiding in N Korea; when the US forces invaded N Korea, they came out of hiding. There are guys who went into hiding to avoid being pressed into N Korean Army. Most of us are teens nearing the military age.

Their Leader Deserts

Jan. 30, 1951—Kojedo: Days have gone by without a word from our commander. We begin to wonder if the man has deserted us. Those who can afford the boat ride to Pusan are deserting us. Ostensibly, they want to look for our vanished leader in Pusan. In order to pay for our food, we collect firewood in the mountains and peddle them in the town market. Those who have rudimentary English get jobs with the American CIC [Counter Intelligence Corps] as interpreters.

I am dejected—my idea of anti-communism crusade did not include physical labor for food. I envy the easy money my seniors are making working for the Americans. Unfortunately my English is not good enough for the job. I devote all of my free time to learning English—it is a matter of life or death for me.

My brother decides to go to Pusan and try his luck there. On the first day in Pusan, he runs into an old school friend from Hamhung and gets a job at a south Korean army hospital. The South Korean Army is acutely short of medical people and anyone with any knowledge of medicine is hired on the spot and pressed into doing surgery and other advanced medical chores.

My brother has only two years of medical education but he doing a surgeon's work at the hospital. He gets free meals and lodging at the hospital in addition to a small stipend. All "doctors" supplement their stipend with a side business—they steal medical supplies and sell them on the black market. Army hospitals are supplied by the Americans and no one feels bad about stealing them. There is plenty more where they came from. My brother is allowed to transfer from Hamhung Medical College to Seoul Medical College (refugee campus in Pusan)—no transcripts necessary.

The Unit Disbands

After a month of waiting, we decide to disband our unit ourselves. Those who are 18 years or older join the S Korean army—the police chief is more than willing to make the arrangement. The under-aged (me included) are sent to the refugee camp at Jisepo. This is how the Student Volunteers Army (Hamhung Unit) met its end.

I learned three years later that our commander did obtain some fund from the Government (Education Ministry) but had decided to keep it for himself. He was discovered hiding among the refugees in Pusan, but there was no criminal charge brought against him. By this time, no one really cared much about the past. All of us are doing what we can to survive.

Feb. 15, 1951—My comrades who joined the S Korean Army land at Samchok (a sea port on the east coast of S Korea) and walk right into an enemy ambush. Few survive. Most of my friends from N Korea perish in a single battle. The poor souls arrive in a single landing craft at Samchok—no covering fire and no scouting.

The commanding officer thinks the town is free of the N Korean Army and orders his men offshore. As soon as the troops are assembled on the beach, the enemy open fire and cut them to pieces. The commanding officer still on the ship abandons his men and escapes. He is later court marshaled and executed for cowardice.

Comrade Kim Ho was a student at Peking University (China) when the war broke out. He was sent home to fight the Americans but, instead, he went AWOL [absent without leave; that is, he deserted] and joined the SVA in 1950. He worked for the US CIC for a number of years and emigrated to US where he earned Ph.D. in history. In 1985, he was killed in a motor cycle accident.

Comrade Park Hong Chul was a student at Kim Il Sung University. He was a captain in the N Korean Army and fought at Inchon. He managed to straggle back to Hamhung and went into hiding. He joined the SVA in November 1950. He worked for the US CIC for three years and graduated from Seoul National University. He taught at a S Korean university until his retirement.

Comrade Chang Suk was a student at Hamhung Medical College when the war broke out. He was a captain (medical) and served in the Nakdong front. He straggled back to Hamhung after the Inchon landing and went into hiding. He joined the SVA and worked for the US CIC for 4 years. He went to Okinawa as an employee of the US State Dept. He retired in America in 1987.

Comrade Kim Ung Sik (my brother) was a student at Hamhung Medical College. He went into hiding when the war broke out to avoid being pressed into the N Korean Army. He was one of the first to join the SVA and one of the staff officers. He joined the S Korean Army Medical Corps at Pusan. He received MD and Ph.D. in Seoul. He held several administrative positions in the ROK Ministry of Health. Upon his retirement, he emigrated to America.

A Civilian Refugee

Feb. 17, 1951—Jisepo: I am officially a civilian refugee. About 91,000 refugees from Hungnam, Hamhung and Wonsan are in the refugee camps at Kojedo. Refugees are housed in US army tents along the beach. They are organized into groups of 10 to 15 families.

Each group designates a group leader who reports to the camp leader. Refugees are fed by the UN Command—each refugee is entitled to daily ration of rice, canned food (GI rations), and other consumer goods. Each family prepares its own meals on the beach.

US army cans are used for cooking rice and soup. Children gather firewood and edibles from the ocean. The ocean provides a host of food—seaweed, clams, oysters and fish. The beach is ideal for cooking food—dried up driftwood make excellent firewood. I run into my neighbors from Hamhung.

Jisepo was a hotbed of the [pro-Communist] Korean People's Committee in 1945. The local peasants and fishermen took over the island from the Japanese on August 15, 1945. The two or three rich landowners who owned all arable land were eliminated along with all Japanese collaborators on the island. The Committee refused to obey the US Military Government's order to disband and fought with arms the invading troops (mostly former Japanese police and army soldiers). Several hundreds of the island's youth were killed and their bodies were thrown into the ocean. Even now, human bones wash up on the beach now and then. Many of the islanders are still bitter and hostile to the Americans and their puppets.

Refugee camps are run by corrupt people (refugees themselves) who pad the camp roster with ghosts. Ghost padding is also practiced by the Korean Militia ('Bang-Wie-Gung'—included many refugees of the military age) and some S Korean army commanders. The UN Command supplies daily rations and military pay based on head counts. The Commander of the Militia (reportedly a former body guard of Dr. Rhee) is executed for corruption.

Refugees are encouraged to leave the camp and become self-supporting as soon as possible. Many refugees start up a business or move to Pusan where opportunities abound for quick-buck schemes. One way in which a corrupt refugee official makes money is not to report those refugees who have left the camp. Rations for non-existent refugees are sold to local residents or to the sole business of Jisepo—a rice wine brewery.

The Dae Kwang School trustees (S Korea) help out the refugee kids by donating funds and teachers for a branch campus in Jisepo. Dae Kwang is funded by rich American and Korean Christians. Tent class rooms are set up on a mountain side. Students and faculty clear a patch of trees and brushes. Tents are donated by the US Army. The principal is a S Korean Christian woman genuinely motivated to educate the refugee kids. Some of the teachers are recruited from refugees. I enroll in the senior class along with 20 others.

Working for the CIC

March 20, 1951—The US CIC (Counter Intelligence Corps) 308th Battalion (Kangnung Unit commanded by a Mr. Adams) sets up a shop in an office at the rice wine brewery. The man in charge is Mr. Chung ("big Ming"), a former Japanese policeman from Hungnam. Mr. Chung reports to an American based in Pusan. Chung's job is to find communist agents hidden among the refugees.

He recruits informants among the refugees for this. Chung is paid by the Americans by the number of "intelligence" reports he sends. I am known as the English "expert" in Jisepo and I offer my service to the CIC. I translate CIC agents reports into English for Mr. Chung. I also translate instructions coming to Mr. Chung into Korean. My pay is the privilege of sleeping in the CIC branch office during the night—if Mr. Chung does not need the room for his frequent affairs with refugee women.

Another form of pay I receive working for Mr. Chung is the dried rice from the brewery. Rice is cooked, dried and then mixed with yeast for fermentation. I get to eat as much of the dried rice as my stomach can hold. In addition, I get to watch Mr. Chung fornicate—he says, it is part of my pay.

I get to be friends with the brewery owner's son (a few years older than I am) who loves to watch the show with me. Not much to do on this island. I have walked around the island several times now and not much new sight-seeing left. I spend about half of my time studying English and the other half talking politics with my fellow refugees.

Working at POW Camps

May 4–20, 1951—A large number of N Korean POWs arrive. They start to build a huge POW camp on the opposite side of the island. All day long the POWs load sand and pebbles on US Army trucks. Several hundred acres of rice fields are filled in for the camp. I look at every POW per chance to find a friend or a relative. One day, I thought I found my father—but it was a false alarm.

Some refugees do find relatives but the US MP's [military police] do not allow any contact. The POWs construct four huge barbed wire enclosures, each of which encloses eight compounds. Some 130,000 Korean prisoners and 20,000 Chinese POWs move in.

June 10, 1951—Kojedo POW Camps: I am employed as an English translator at the POW camp. A compound consists of 30 to 40 tents, each tent housing 30–60 POWs. Each compound is enclosed by high wire fence with watch towers here and there. The entrance is guarded by 5 to 6 US soldiers. Communist officers are isolated from soldiers. Chinese POW's are separated from N Korean POWs.

There are camps for "civilian internees"—those S Koreans who joined the Korean militia. Female POWs are segregated from male POWs. Each camp is run by the POWs themselves, but communist cadres manage to set 'under-tent' tunnels to control the whole camp.

Five of my former comrades of the Student Volunteers Army have been working at the camp site (The US CIC has an office here) since January of 1951. I am happy to be reunited with them. They share a tiny room rented from a farmer with two Chinese agents from Taiwan. The agents handle the Chinese POWs. They are fluent in English and Japanese. They say that the Japanese treated Formosans [Taiwanese] fairly and that they miss the Japanese colonials. It is obvious that these Chinese are Jap lovers.

My work consists of translating POW profiles (name, address, unit designation, educational background, etc.) into English. There are about 15 of us. Our office is an army tent and we share it with American GI's who edit our English. POWs are brought in 15 (one per translator) at a time and fill out a standard form in Korean. We are popular with the refugees looking to see if any of their relatives are POW's. We are not allowed to look through the files but we manage to locate POW relatives now and then. The relatives bring food and family news to us and we smuggle them to the POWs.

Mistreatment of Koreans by Americans

American GI's cuss, kick and mistreat the POWs. It is painful to watch our fellow Koreans treated like animals by foreigners—but there is not much we can do. We are treated no better than the POWs. GI's love to play dirty tricks on the gooks. They would throw down a cigarette butt on the floor when a POW is close by. Some POWs stoop down, pick up the butt and puff on it. The GI's take photos and laugh. Another popular trick is to leave candy bars or other tempting items around. When a poor soul grabs it, the GI's pounce on him—"We caught this gook stealing this or that."

Jan. 21, 1952—My career at the POW camp comes to an abrupt end. All translators have to wear US GI fatigues and the army cap. As we enter our office tent, we leave our cap on a table. The American GI's do the same. All caps look alike. I make the mistake of picking up a wrong cap. The GI's set up a trap for me and I am caught in their trap. They accuse me of stealing the cap and I am fired on the spot.

Korea Was Devastated by the War

Y.T. Pyun

The Korean War caused widespread devastation throughout Korea, but especially in South Korea, where the bulk of the fighting took place. All but two South Korean cities were attacked and at least partially destroyed, and thousands of villages were burned to the ground, thus turning millions of villagers into refugees. Crop failures caused by war, drought, and lack of fertilizer inflated the price of rice, Koreans' dietary staple, putting it beyond the means of millions of Koreans, leading to mass starvation. The South Korean government could do little to combat these problems as its resources were almost totally committed to combating the Communists. To survive as a nation and as a people, South Korea desperately needed billions of dollars of foreign aid.

Y.T. (Yung Tai) Pyun was the minister of foreign affairs for the Republic of Korea (ROK, or South Korea) from 1951 to 1955. The following viewpoint is taken from Pyun's statement to the United Nations regarding a report by the UN Committee for the Unification and Rehabilitation of Korea (UNCURK) shortly before the end of the war. Pyun attempts to convey how truly appalling the conditions in South Korea are as a result of the war. He also calls on the international community to provide massive aid to Korea because, he argues, the war is an international conflict.

As ROK foreign minister, Y.T. Pyun would go on to negotiate the armistice that ended hostilities in July 1953. South Korea would get the Western aid Pyun lobbied for, but with strings attached: The Mutual Defense Treaty Between the Republic of Korea and the United States, signed in October 1953 by Pyun and U.S. secretary of state John Foster Dulles, granted the United States ongoing rights to station land, air, and naval forces in and

Y.T. Pyun, statement before the First Political and Security Committee of the United Nations, November 3, 1952.

around South Korean territory. This concession gave the U.S. military an important Asian base of operations throughout the Cold War.

M r. Chairman, I have so recently arrived from Korea that I have not yet been able to push into the background of my mind the awful scenes of misery and suffering in which I have lived during the twenty-eight months of this war, and amidst which my people are now entering upon the third winter of their terrible ordeal. I cannot speak to you here in these comfortable surroundings without the vivid memories of the conditions in my homeland being ever present in my thoughts. Indeed, I do not think it would be proper for us to discuss this question without a very sharp awareness of what it means to the millions of human beings who are so desperatcly involved. I cannot escape the feeling that if by some means the scene of this meeting could be transferred for a few days to Pusan or to Seoul, our deliberations might take on a heightened realism and a sharper insistence upon a speedy and effective decision.

During the period of this war we have suffered a devastation and ruination of our homeland such as perhaps no other people in history have had to endure. Our national capital, Seoul—a city which is dear to our hearts and which housed more than a million and a half of our people—has been captured and recaptured four separate times. For more than fifteen months Seoul has sprawled upon its site in a shambles of ruin, a grim memorial of the terror that has swept over us.

Korean Cities and Villages Have Been Shattered

Fifty-three of our fifty-five large cities are totally or partially destroyed. Twelve hundred of our five thousand villages have been seared and burned. More than ten million people in the south have lost their homes or their possessions. More than a hundred thousand of our children have been orphaned. Multimillions of our people are casualties of the conflict, of hunger and disease, or are helpless victims driven into captivity by the cruel and cynical invaders of our homeland. And every single Korean who remains alive today bears in his mind and on his person the scars of this terrible conflict—the searing memory of loved ones lost, the blight of hunger and cold and disease, the suffering from a paralyzing inflation that steals away our last means of livelihood and spreads the suffering of the war into every home.

The living standards of the Korean people have sharply declined since the outbreak of the war—dipping and falling daily and visibly until they have now fallen below the subsistence level. In the outlying rural places, beyond the reach of the foreign observers, thousands of people are actually vanishing out of existence quietly, like so many sparrows, unseen, unrelieved. This must not be allowed to happen anywhere, and far less in the only country in which an actual war of a global nature is being fought. This must not be allowed to happen especially among the population from which the bulk of combat manpower has to be drawn.

The patience of the Korean people has been praised. But there must be a limit to their patience, as there is to all things human. Observers have called their patience a miracle. But miracles don't just happen every day. Before their patience reaches the limit, before miracles do stop, something must be done and that quickly. At this very moment I seem to see millions of my mute fellow countrymen raising their emaciated arms as though to signal the message, "We hate Communism more than all these sufferings, but, oh, in the name of heaven, do not drive us to extremities!" . . .

Little Progress Has Been Made Toward Recovery

Now let us turn to Chapter III of the report, dealing with the economic and financial situation. In paragraph 183 the report summarizes, "In short, despite the improvement that has occurred, the economy of the country is still suffering greatly from the war and has still not taken a major step forward toward recovery."

Mr. Chairman, I submit that this is an understatement which requires considerable elaboration if your Committee is to have an adequate understanding of the miserable situation in which my countrymen exist.

There has, says the report, been no "major step forward toward recovery." Can you picture the meaning of this phrase in terms of six hundred thousand homes destroyed—and only 25,000 or so rebuilt? Can you see what it means in terms of seventy per cent of our textile plants destroyed, with only 88,000 spindles now in use out of our 316,000? Can you visualize what would be the effect in terms of suffering and privation in your own families, if you were confronted, as we are, by price increases on scarce but vital foodstuffs and clothing of fifteen times and more?

Mr. Chairman, we have recently read in the newspapers that a new agency is to be sent to our country to conduct yet another survey and to make yet another report on the extent of our war damage and on the nature of our needs for rehabilitation. Thus far, Sir, there have been many surveys and many reports, but tragically little reconstruction. The struggle in our country is often called a Limited War, but for Korea it is an unlimited war of total destruction. It is often called the Korean War, but this is another misnomer, for it actually is a global war that is being waged at its hottest on our soil. Had Korea been a piece of barren unpopulated rock, the Communists would have taken it all the same to use it as a base, from which to rip up the Pacific traffic of the free world and the free world would have had to defend it, minus the patriotic and self-sacrificing Korean people. More than 15 billion American dollars have already gone into the waging of this war of destruction. Compared with that huge sum the three

A young boy stands amidst the rubble of his home in Seoul. South Korea experienced widespread devastation during the war. © Bettmann CORBIS

hundred millions spent thus far for relief and rehabilitation since the war started are far from adequate to cover all the phases of nationwide relief. It is true that much has been done for Korean relief, which we gratefully acknowledge and take to heart. But it is also true that a whole country laid waste is something more than can adequately be remedied by usual measures of relief and rehabilitation.

Honorable delegates of the Committee, I wish it were possible to take you in a body to the blasted battlefield of my country and to conduct you through the scenes of destruction and misery. Refugees, war-sufferers and those whom the conflict has rendered destitute are numbered in paragraph 185 of the report at 10,406,000. Of this total, 4,972,000 receive full or partial relief. This means that the submerged 5,434,000 receive no aid whatsoever. This cold, unrecognized number represents all shades of human tragedy, hunger, destitution and misery. This ominously neglected number breaks down into countless famished families and uprooted individuals, many feeding on barks and grasses, whose sad tale nobody tells and who suffer unseen. What shall we do about these miserable waifs of the war? Is it right that young men should go to the front leaving their fathers and mothers, their brothers and sisters, with bloated faces and swollen bellies, feeding on grass? Is it right to turn the wounded veterans of this global conflict out of our make-shift hospitals before their wounds are healed, in order to make room for fresh contingents of their wounded comrades?

Crop Failures Mean Inflation and Starvation

Last year the crops were poor. Partly this is a result of the destruction and losses of the war and of shortage of fertilizer. But the crop estimates were rationalized to accord with the limitations of aid. So we had a rice famine this year, with the price of rice leaping up to ten times its level last year. This year the drought has been more general, and was followed by long rains and withering winds. Our expectation is for a much smaller crop than was harvested a year ago. Experts say that about one million tons of rice must be imported in order to prevent widespread starvation. This means that one 10,000-ton freighter must carry to us a capacity cargo of rice every three days during the forthcoming food year. Is the required grain purchased somewhere, ready to be shipped in? Are the ships chartered for the regular carrying of the grain? Are storage facilities going to be built throughout South Korea in order that this grain may not go to waste? Are there going to be civilian means of transportation, including trucks, to move the grain swiftly from place to place?

My country, Sir, is an extreme case of all round anemia. The war destroyed the bulk of our beasts of burden. Ox carts are seldom seen. The sad fact is that most of the vehicles on the roads are military, and very few belong to individuals or can be used by the Government for civilian purposes. The bottleneck in transportation is the worst handicap of all.

In paragraphs 178, 179 and 183, the report indicates that the Republic of Korea Government is to be blamed for failure to take adequate steps to deal with these economic problems. Paragraph 179 concludes, "Therefore, resolute and effective action by the Government of the Republic of Korea to get inflation under control would be a major step forward in the reconstruction of the country."

We are puzzled, Sir, for the Commission knows that the Government lacks the essential prerequisites for such a nationwide economic control. If resolute and effective action by the Government were all that was required to bring inflation under control, it would have been controlled long ago. More than a year ago the Government stopped issuing banknotes for internal consumption and forced its military and relief ministries to operate as best they could on a balanced budget. But for the past two years the Government has been issuing more than a billion *won* [the Korean monetary unit] notes daily as a loan to the United Nations forces. The result is that some seventy per cent of all the currency in circulation is accounted for by this loan. The basic remedy lies and must lie, however, in the rehabilitation of the ruined factories so as to produce sufficient consumer goods to meet the needs, or, pending this reconstruction, to bring in the same amount of consumer goods from abroad. This remedy contemplates an aid program on an enormous scale far beyond anything previously known. Inflation in Korea is, properly, an international problem, just as the war is an international undertaking.

The World Must Do More to Help

Nothing can shatter the aggressive solidarity of world Communism except the spontaneous solidarity of all the free peoples throughout the world, demonstrating their willingness to bear an equal share in the suffering and the danger. Cooperation can scarcely be fruitful in the end if the country to which the war is limited must accept a total sacrifice while many other free nations are content with only a token sacrifice. If what has happened to Korea is allowed to lie unrelieved and unrehabilitated, it will remain as a ruin of collective action, discouraging all free nations on the periphery of the Communist Empire from actively supporting the collective action of the free world.

This is a gloomy picture, but, thank God, the means of erasing it still lies in the power of the free peoples of the world, if and when they accept a greater degree of solidarity and a fuller share of sacrifice. Then and only then will there arise a permanent and triumphant evidence to future generations that Korea was saved by collective action, and that through this victory for collective security a decisive victory was won in Korea for the salvation of human civilization.

The Fifty-Year Division of Korean Society

Stephanie Strom

One of the tragedies of the Korean War is the forced separation of families by the Demilitarized Zone (DMZ), the two-and-a-half-mile-wide unoccupied zone running west to east along the 38th parallel that was negotiated as the boundary between North and South Korea in 1953. As in any civil war, many families were divided because their members chose to support opposing sides. Most family division during the Korean War, however, seems to have been caused simply because family members were living on both sides of the DMZ when the border was enforced. Unlike the Berlin Wall, which separated families living in East and West Berlin in 1961, the barriers that were erected along the DMZ by both North and South Korea were devoid of checkpoints where family members could cross over to the other side to visit their relatives. As a result, for fifty years many Koreans lived without knowing what had become of their parents, siblings, or other close relatives.

In 2000, the fiftieth anniversary of the outbreak of the Korean War, North Korea's leader, Kim Jong Il, permitted about one hundred North Korean families to fly to Seoul, South Korea, for the first of several state-planned family reunions. Kim claimed to be motivated by a desire to work for the peaceful reunification of Korea. Most experts, however, saw the reunions as a bid by Kim to make his regime appear less totalitarian and more humane in the eyes of the world.

New York Times reporter Stephanie Strom covered the first family reunion of North and South Koreans on August 15, 2000. In this viewpoint Strom reports that though the event clearly had political overtones and elements of staging for public rela-

tions purposes, the reunion was primarily characterized by genuine emotion and Koreans' willingness to reconcile their countries' differences.

Under the watchful gaze of North Korean minders, 100 families separated for the last five decades today began the arduous process of rebuilding relationships torn apart by war.

In one heart-rending scene after another, mothers embraced children long given up for dead, brothers and sisters struggled to identify adults they knew until now only as children, wives steeled themselves to meet husbands long since wedded to other spouses, and vice versa.

"Thank you so much for being alive!" Hong Ghil Soon, 87, exclaimed as she embraced her daughter, Kim Ok Bae, who arrived this morning on the first North Korean plane to land on South Korean soil since 1950. "Thank the dear leader for taking such good care of you!"

Kim Jong Il Arranges a Reunion

The "dear leader" is Kim Jong Il, the North Korean leader whose surprisingly sophisticated political maneuvering underlay all the drama. Here was a South Korean mother whose daughter was effectively kidnapped by North Korean troops during the war heaping praise on the man whose father, Kim Il Sung, led those troops and founded the totalitarian state that split her family apart, and who until recently was himself seen by the world outside as a reclusive, dictatorial oddity.

The plane that brought the 100 people south today carried another 100 people north on its return trip for similar reunions. They were accompanied by some South Korean staff members, but without the mandate to monitor the reunions that the North's minders apparently had. The reunions today are the first in what South Korean officials hope will be a series of three sets of family gatherings this year.

Kim Jong Il, who met with South Korean news executives last week, told them that he intended to arrange two more re-unions, in September and October. Southern officials say the planning for those gatherings is already in the works.

The meetings are part of a strategy, mapped out by Kim Jong Il and the South Korean president, Kim Dae Jung, in their historic meeting in June, to begin the process of reunifying the two countries by breaking down the barriers that divide their people.

Already North Korea has agreed to re-establish rail links between the two countries, and last week it signed an agreement with one of South Korea's biggest conglomerates to develop a permanent meeting place for separated families at Kaesong, just north of the border.

Kim Jong Il has even said he would like to find a way to allow visiting relatives to stay in each other's homes, rather than meet in convention centers and hotel rooms as they are doing now. But those taking part in these reunions clearly cared not a whit that they have become political pawns. They were simply happy to be families once again.

The vast convention hall where the meetings took place today reverberated with shouts of joy and peals of happy laughter, not to mention a fair amount of relieved sobbing, as families solved long-standing mysteries and confirmed or discarded long-held suspicions.

Discovering What Happened to Mother

For five decades Moon Kyung Ja wondered what happened to her mother, who was thrown in jail for aiding the North Korean Army during the Korean War and was never seen again.

Today she got her answer from her eldest sister, Moon Yang Ok, whom she had not seen since the war and had at times presumed dead. Their mother did not die in jail, as

Moon Kyung Ja feared, but instead escaped and walked to safety in North Korea with her two oldest daughters and baby son.

"Mother passed away without fulfilling her dream of seeing you," Moon Yang Ok told her sister while stroking her face. "But your brother and sister are alive."

"Oh, my God, they are alive!" Moon Kyung Ja shouted, throwing her hands in the air. "My family is alive!"

Her sister hugged her hard. "Let me see you," she said. "Let me see your face. I have learned how long a day is, waiting this last week to see you."

Hopes are high that these are the first steps toward a more sweeping reconciliation, including greater economic cooperation and decreased military tension between the two countries, which are technically still at war.

But how far the current thaw will go remains to be seen. North Korea was careful to arrange an insurance policy against defections, making sure that the South Koreans who have gone north will not leave until all of the North Korean family members are home.

And a South Korean official said today that his country fully expected to pay the impoverished North for these reunions. Already, the South Korean government has given each family $500 to give to its visiting relatives from the North.

North Koreans Seem Surprisingly Prosperous

The North Koreans who arrived today all appear to be members of the country's elite: professors, doctors, artists and the like. During interviews a few mentioned that they had been "chosen by the dear leader" to make the trip, suggesting that they have ties to the North Korean political hierarchy.

They were in high spirits, waving and clapping as they left the plane, and seemed more affluent than their South Korean relatives had expected. Many South Koreans had bought watches to give their relatives, but many of the visitors arrived wearing nice watches. Two or three of the seven North Korean women wore exquisite—and expensive—han dok, traditional Korean dresses.

Nonetheless, some of the delegation's spit and polish seemed a bit contrived. Several men seemed to be wearing identical suits and identical ties, and none of them carried any hand luggage on the plane, in stark contrast to the South Koreans who went north nearly staggering under tote bags jammed with gifts.

Questions about what the visitors from the North thought of Seoul were ignored or brushed aside, and the visitors took every opportunity to praise the dear leader and the great leader, as Kim Il Sung, the founder of North Korea, was known.

Moon Yang Ok proudly showed her sister a handsome watch with "Kim Il Sung" written in elegant red calligraphy across its light silver face. "I received this as an award for my academic achievements from the great leader," she said proudly.

She teaches medicine, as does their younger brother, who was 2 when they fled for the North. "Thanks to our great leader, we have become medical professionals and my younger brother is the leading academic at the Hamheung University School of Medicine," she said. "There aren't many people like that."

She said her brother had invented a machine to treat arteriosclerosis.

But others were more unsettled by the attention they received today. "My sister seems really nervous," said Kim Suk Bae, whose sister, Kim Ok Bae, arrived in Seoul today. "Whenever the men from the other side come by, the ones with badges, she keeps praising the dear leader and tells us to do the same. We feel like we have to play along, because if we don't, something bad might happen to her when she returns to her home."

Kim Ok Bae turned her head away whenever she was asked a question, so her sister answered for her. She said Kim Ok Bae left their house in September 1950 on a school trip to perform for North Korean troops. The performance was so good that the North Koreans "recruited" the performers to travel around and keep morale high.

After the war, Kim Ok Bae became an anatomy professor, her sister said. She is married to another anatomy professor and has two children, a son who is a movie producer and a daughter who is a teacher.

Her sister said Kim Ok Bae had told the family that every year on her mother's birthday, she prepared a birthday feast, set a beautiful table and celebrated by herself. "I have lived until now with the guilt of having been a bad daughter," Kim Ok Bae said to her mother, Hong Ghil Soon, who is 87, when they met today.

"But you've turned out wonderfully!" her mother exclaimed.

Indeed, in many cases the North Korean visitors seemed better off than their southern relatives, which is probably precisely the message Kim Jong Il wished to send. Kim Hyun Ki remembered his older brother, Kim Hyun Suk, who disappeared from school shortly after the war started, as a bright, handsome, engaging youngster.

Today, Kim Hyun Suk did indeed seem to be all of those things—and much younger than his two younger brothers. A tall man with a thick head of salt-and-pepper hair, he spoke animatedly during their meeting.

"I went into the army for three years, and after that I went to college," he said. "They sent me to college to study engineering, and I studied really hard, father."

He said his three children also had college degrees. No one in his South Korean family, which found it difficult to scratch out a living here once the authorities found out they had a family in the North, can make a similar statement.

An Older Brother Apologizes for His Father's Death

Kim Dong Man was not about to let his brother Kim Dong Jin forget the hard times his ideological beliefs had brought upon his family. Kim Dong Jin joined the North Korean Army after being jailed several times for his Communist beliefs.

The South Korean Army then threw his father into prison because of his son's activities and confiscated all of the family's possessions, Kim Dong Man said. "My father died because of my older brother," he said.

Kim Dong Jin, a retired civil servant, sat silently as his brother described the family's woes. "He still hasn't told me what he did for a living in the North," Kim Dong Man said. "But he did say he lives in a 100-square-yard house, and from that I know he's wealthy."

Kim Dong Jin then broke his silence. "I feel like a rich man today because I am able to see my family again," he said quietly. "But if I would have stayed in the south, I would have died.

"When I was 24 and the North Koreans took me in, all I had were my two fists. But the great leader educated me and gave me a job."

For his part, Kim Dong Man says he holds no grudges against his brother. "Older brother told me he is sorry," he said. "These tragedies happened because we lost our country to the Japanese and then fought ourselves after that. My brother was part of that. I want all of this suffering to end with my generation."

Chronology

1905

Korea becomes a Japanese protectorate.

1910

Japan annexes Korea.

1941

December 7: Japanese attack U.S. naval base at Pearl Harbor, Hawaii, bringing the United States into World War II and beginning the war in the Pacific.

1943

December 3: Cairo Declaration pledges American, British, and Chinese support for Korean independence after World War II ends.

1945

February: Yalta Conference between Allied leaders yields informal agreement to establish a four-power trusteeship (American, British, Chinese, and Soviet) for Korea.

July: Potsdam Declaration reaffirms the four powers' support for Korean independence as outlined in Cairo Declaration.

August 9: USSR, a late entry in the Pacific war, sends troops into Korea.

August 11: U.S. General Order No. 1 provides that Japanese forces in Korea north of the 38th parallel surrender to Soviet troops while Japanese forces south of the 38th parallel surrender to U.S. troops.

September 8: U.S. troops enter Korea.

December: Moscow Conference creates a four-power trusteeship for Korea and establishes a Joint U.S.–USSR Commission to settle the issue of Korean unification.

1946

September: U.S. representatives present the unresolved issue of Korean unification to the United Nations; UN passes a resolution calling for general elections, the establishment of a national assembly and government, and the removal of all foreign troops.

1948

May 10: General elections are held in South Korea.

August 15: Republic of Korea (ROK) is established in South Korea.

August 25: General elections are held in North Korea.

September 9: Democratic People's Republic of Korea (DPRK) is established in North Korea.

October 12: USSR recognizes DPRK as the only legal government in Korea.

December: Soviet troops leave DPRK.

December 12: UN recognizes ROK as the only legal government in Korea.

1949

March: USSR grants military aid to DPRK.

June: U.S. troops leave ROK.

October: U.S. grants military aid to ROK.

1950

June 25: North Korean People's Army (NKPA) invades ROK.

June 27: U.S. and UN pledge military support for ROK.

June 28: NKPA captures Seoul, South Korea's capital.

July 1: First U.S. ground troops arrive in Korea.

July 3: NKPA captures Inchon.

September: U.S. forces conduct amphibious landing at Inchon, drive NKPA from Pusan, recapture Seoul.

October: ROK troops cross 38th parallel into North Korea; capture Wonsan and Pyongyang, the North Korean capital; engage Communist Chinese Forces (CCF) at Unsan and reach Yalu River, the border between North Korea and China.

November: U.S. troops engage CCF at Unsan; CCF forces U.S. retreat from Chosin Reservoir.

December 26: Gen. Matthew Ridgway assumes command of U.S. troops in Korea.

1951

January: CCF captures Seoul; U.S. troops abandon Inchon to CCF occupation, then mount counterattack.

February 10: U.S. troops retake Inchon.

March 14: U.S. troops retake Seoul.

April: Ridgway replaces Gen. Douglas MacArthur as commander of UN forces; CCF and NKPA launch counterattack, halted by U.S. and ROK troops on the outskirts of Seoul.

June 23: USSR calls for armistice talks.

July 10: Armistice talks begin at Kaesong.

August 23: Communists break off negotiations.

October: U.S. troops capture Heartbreak Ridge; armistice talks resume at Panmunjom.

November 12: U.S. troops halt offensive, strengthen defensive lines along the 38th parallel.

1952

October 8: UN calls for end to armistice talks, citing lack of progress.

1953

April 26: Armistice talks resume.

July 6–11: CCF defeat U.S. troops at Pork Chop Hill.

July 27: Armistice signed; military line between ROK and DPRK troops replaces the 38th parallel as the official boundary between North and South Korea.

For Further Research

Books

Bevin Alexander, *Korea: The First War We Lost*. New York: Hippocrene, 2000.

Otto F. Apel and Pat Apel, *MASH: An Army Surgeon in Korea*. Lexington: University Press of Kentucky, 1998.

David J. Bercuson, *Blood in the Hills: The Canadian Army in the Korean War*. Toronto: University of Toronto Press, 1999.

William T. Bowers, William M. Hammond, and George L. MacGarrigle, *Black Soldier, White Army: The 24th Infantry Regiment in Korea*. Washington, DC: Center of Military History, U.S. Army, 1996.

James Brady, *The Coldest War: A Memoir of Korea*. New York: Thomas Dunne, 1990.

Choong Soon Kim, *Faithful Endurance: An Ethnography of Korean Family Dispersal*. Tucson: University of Arizona Press, 1988.

Bruce Cumings, *Korea's Place in the Sun: A Modern History*. New York: W.W. Norton, 1997.

Paul M. Edwards, *A Guide to Films on the Korean War*. Westport, CT: Greenwood, 1997.

George Forty, *At War in Korea*. London: Arms and Armour, 1997.

Alexander L. George, *The Chinese Communist Army in Action: The Korean War and Its Aftermath*. New York: Columbia University Press, 1967.

Sergei N. Goncharov et al., *Uncertain Partners: Stalin, Mao, and the Korean War*. Stanford, CA: Stanford University Press, 1993.

Jeffrey Grey, *The Commonwealth Armies and the Korean War: An Alliance Study.* Manchester, England: Manchester University Press, 1988.

Michael E. Haas, *In the Devil's Shadow: UN Special Operations During the Korean War.* Annapolis, MD: Naval Institute Press, 2000.

Michael Hickey, *The Korean War: The West Confronts Communism.* Woodstock, NY: Overlook, 2000.

William B. Hopkins, *One Bugle, No Drums: The Marines at Chosin Reservoir.* Chapel Hill, NC: Algonquin, 1986.

Edwin Hoyt, *The Bloody Road to Panmunjom.* New York: Stein and Day, 1985.

Kim Chul Baum and James I. Matray, *Korea and the Cold War: Division, Destruction, and Disarmament.* Claremont, CA: Regina, 1993.

Kim Il Sung, *For the Independent Peaceful Reunification of Korea.* New York: International, 1975.

Peter Lowe, *The Origins of the Korean War.* New York: Longman, 1997.

Ben O'Dowd, *In Valiant Company.* St. Lucia, Queensland, Australia: University of Queensland Press, 2000.

Y.T. Pyun, *Korea: My Country.* Washington, DC: Korean Pacific, 1953.

Milton J. Rosen, *An American Rabbi in Korea: A Chaplain's Journey in the Forgotten War.* Tuscaloosa: University of Alabama Press, 2004.

Harry Spiller, ed., *American POWs in Korea: Sixteen Personal Accounts.* Jefferson, NC: McFarland, 1998.

William Stueck, *The Korean War: An International History.* Princeton, NJ: Princeton University Press, 1995.

John Toland, *In Mortal Combat: Korea, 1950–1953*. New York: Morrow, 1991.

Spencer C. Tucker, ed., *Encyclopedia of the Korean War: A Political, Social, and Military History*. Santa Barbara, CA: ABC-CLIO, 2000.

Richard Whelan, *Drawing the Line: The Korean War, 1950–1953*. Boston: Little, Brown, 1990.

Xiaobing Li et al., eds., *Mao's Generals Remember Korea*. Lawrence: University Press of Kansas, 2001.

Web Sites

Mt. Holyoke College, "The Korean War Web Resources." (www.mtholyoke.edu/acad/intrel/korea/korea.htm). The site contains links to valuable essays about various aspects of the war and its causes, to primary sources such as telegrams and memoranda from leaders of both sides, and to other excellent Web sites about the war.

U.S. Center for Military History, Army, "Remembering the Korean War." (www.army.mil/cmh-pg/reference/Korea/kw-remem.htm). An archive of U.S. military records that includes links to official histories, studies, and documents, and profiles of recipients of the Congressional Medal of Honor. Of particular interest are links to illustrations and images of the Korean War, including battlefield photographs and war-related posters.

Young Sik Kim, "Eyewitness: A North Korean Remembers," KIMSOFT. (www.kimsoft.com/korea/eyewit.htm). A fascinating memoir by a North Korean refugee who fought against the North Korean army in the Korean War. Offers an eye-opening view of refugee and prisoner-of-war camps and the workings of U.S. intelligence networks.

Index